VEGAN in 7

DELICIOUS PLANT-BASED RECIPES IN 7 INGREDIENTS OR FEWER

☆ ☆ ☆ ☆ ☆ ☆ ☆

RITA SERANO

PHOTOGRAPHRY BY LAURA EDWARDS

KYLE BOOKS

Published in 2018 by Kyle Books
www.kylebooks.com

Distributed by National Book Network
4501 Forbes Blvd, Suite 200,
Lanham, MD 20706
Phone: (800) 462-6420
Fax: (800) 338-4550
customercare@nbnbooks.com

First published in Great Britain in 2017 by
Kyle Books, an imprint of Kyle Cathie Ltd.

10 9 8 7 6 5 4 3 2 1

ISBN 978-1-909487-85-7

Editor: Claire Rogers
Copy Editor: Anne McDowall
Editorial Adaptation: Jennifer Duardo
Proofreader: Vicki Murrell
Designer: Georgia Vaux
Photographer: Laura Edwards
Food Stylist: Joss Herd
Prop Stylist: Tabitha Hawkins
Production: Nic Jones and Gemma John

Library of Congress Control Number: 2017953514

Color reproduction by ALTA London
Printed and bound in China by C&C
Offset Printing Co., Ltd.

INTRODUCTION

I must have been about six years old when I first cooked a meal for my parents. It was a simple one – pasta with tomato sauce – but I remember how proud I was and how much joy I felt making it. That was the start of many meals: I still find joy in cooking for family and friends.

As a child, I was raised on a macrobiotic diet, eating brown rice with beans, veggies, and some sesame seeds on top – loads of whole-grain, wholesome food made with fresh produce. Although I occasionally ate sweets at my grandparents' home, this was an exception: real sweet treats were fruits. My father would come home with the most delicious mangoes, which we shared immediately, and I remember eating gooseberries plucked straight from the bush in my grandfather's garden.

But my journey to healthy eating has not all been smooth sailing. As happens with many children, my diet went awry when I reached puberty. Although I was still eating a mainly vegetarian diet, it was not a healthy one as, with my friends, I indulged in chips, fried food, cheese, carbonated drinks, chocolate, and a whole lot of other "edible substances." It wasn't long before my poor eating habits took their toll: I developed red patches all over my body. The doctors told me it was psoriasis, an autoimmune disease, and that I would have to learn to live with it.

I decided to improve my eating, so went back on a macrobiotic diet and took cooking lessons. But the patches wouldn't go away. Then I started Kung Fu training and met a teacher who helped me get back on the right track. I eliminated all processed food, animal food, and refined sugars; my liking for fresh foods, especially fruits, grew and I also did body cleanses with herbs and juice fasts. Quite soon, the patches started to fade and I had more energy. I felt light and healthy.

Around 2001, I got into raw food. It was not an easy diet to follow at that time as many raw food diet essentials, such as chia seeds, were hard to find. However, I was so inspired by eating, preparing, and teaching raw food that I even went to New York to eat at raw food restaurants, which did not really exist in Europe then. After seven years eating raw food, I gradually began to reintroduce warm cooked meals in my diet again. I was missing them, especially in wintertime when it was cold. However, my diet remained a plant-based one.

When I became pregnant, healthy eating took on even more importance: there was a new life growing inside me that was feeding whatever I put in my mouth! During the pregnancy, and when I was breastfeeding, I was highly aware of what I was eating, but it didn't stop there. From the moment my daughter took her first bites of food, I wanted to make sure she would have the very best of what nature has to offer. Even when she was little, I let her choose vegetables and fruits when we were in the organic store or market. And when vegetables were growing in my garden, she picked the ripe berries or pulled carrots out of the ground. Helping her prepare food was another great way to get her involved in the whole food process. Nowadays, she refuses to eat refined foods like crisps. She doesn't crave sugar: for her, fruits are the best sweets around.

I remain convinced that a plant-based diet is best for me – and, I believe, most beneficial for others and for the planet, as well. I choose food that is local, in season, and in its most natural state. I want to eat as clean as possible, which means organic. (I was once told that apples are sprayed 28 times before picking them! That doesn't make sense to me.)

Sitting down at the table should be a joyful moment and food should always taste delicious – a celebration of what nature has to offer. I like to surprise guests with dishes that don't contain anything but good food! There are so many examples of plant-based dishes from around the world that you can cook. People have been eating this way for hundreds, maybe thousands of years, so there's a lot to discover.

I want to show you that cooking and eating wholesome, vegan food is easy, fun, and delicious. Beans, grains, vegetables, fruits, and nuts never have to be boring, neither does good food have to be complicated. To prove the point, none of the recipes here contains more than seven ingredients, plus the kitchen essentials of salt, pepper, and occasionally a little oil. My hope is that you will use this book as an inspiration for your everyday cooking. Whether you're a committed vegan or simply want to explore plant-based food; whether you are wanting to eat wholesome vegan food for health, animal-welfare, or environmental reasons – or just want something new and delicious on your plate, I invite you to get inspired, get cooking, and have fun!

★ **START** ☆ FAST ☆ FRESH ☆ NOURISH ☆ GATHER ☆ SWEET ☆ BASIC

SMOOTHIES

Smoothies are a very quick way of upping your fruit and vedge intake and the perfect breakfast solution if you don't have much of an appetite in the morning. Also for a between-meals snack, or if you're craving something delicious on the run. If you like smoothies less dense, just add a little extra liquid. You can also top with extra fruit, nuts, or granola to make them even more substantial.

PURPLE POWER

Serves 2–3

☆	☆	☆	☆	☆	☆	☆
2 ripe bananas, peeled and cut into chunks	1½ cups fresh or frozen blueberries or blackberries	A handful of spinach	Juice of ½ lemon	2 to 3 cups almond or cashew milk, depending on how thick you want your smoothie	1 tablespoon acai powder (optional)	A few drops of stevia, for a sweeter taste (optional)

Place all the ingredients in a blender and process on high speed until completely smooth. Pour into glasses, or bowls if thicker, and add your toppings of choice.

ORANGE BOOST

Serves 2–3

☆	☆	☆	☆	☆	☆	☆
2 oranges, peeled and segmented	1 fresh mango, peeled, stoned and cut into chunks	2 teaspoons freshly grated ginger	2 teaspoons freshly grated turmeric, or 1 teaspoon dried turmeric	Pinch of chilli powder	2 to 3 cups coconut water (or water), depending on the desired thickness	A few drops of stevia (optional)

Place all the ingredients in a blender and process on high speed until completely smooth. Pour into glasses, or bowls if thicker, and add your toppings of choice (see page 10).

SUPER GREEN

Serves 2–3

☆	☆	☆	☆	☆	☆	☆
3 ripe pears, peeled, cored and cut into chunks	1 ripe banana, peeled and cut into chunks	½ ripe avocado, peeled, pitted, and cut into chunks	A large handful of kale	1 tablespoon chopped fresh mint	Juice of 1 lime	2½ cups coconut water

Place all the ingredients in a blender and process on high speed until completely smooth. Pour into glasses, or bowls if thicker, and add your toppings of choice (see below).

★ Variation
Add 1 tablespoon of spirulina or other favorite greens to make this smoothie even healthier.

CLASSIC RED

Serves 2–3

☆	☆	☆	☆	☆	☆
½ cup fresh or frozen strawberries	½ cup fresh or frozen raspberries	2 ripe bananas, peeled and cut into chunks	2 to 3 cups almond milk, depending on how thick you want your smoothie	½ teaspoon vanilla powder or extract	A few drops of stevia (optional)

Place all the ingredients in a blender and process on high speed until completely smooth. Pour into glasses, or bowls if thicker, and add your toppings of choice (see below).

★ Optional extras
You can top these smoothies with extra fruit, nuts, or granola to make them even more substantial.

MUESLI HOW I LIKE IT

I first tried muesli in Switzerland as a teenager, but I didn't like it – I thought it was a far too dry and unappetizing way to start the day. Years later, I read about Bircher Brenner, who invented Bircher Muesli and used it in his health clinic. To get the maximum health benefits from his muesli, he recommended soaking it the night before. This makes such a difference in taste! Feel free to experiment with different ingredients – but always leave them to soak overnight.

Makes 1 large jar, approx 1 ½ lb.

☆	☆	☆	☆	☆	☆	☆
4 cups rye flakes	1 cup dried cranberries (make sure they don't contain added sugar)	¼ cup chia seeds	1 cup coconut flakes	⅓ cup raw pistachio nuts, shelled	2 teaspoons aniseed	Apple juice, to serve

Mix all the dry muesli ingredients together. You can store this mixture in an airtight container for up to 2 months.

The day before you want to eat the muesli, combine about ½ cup of the dry mixture with ⅔ apple juice for each serving, then leave in the fridge overnight to soak.

★ Variations
Substitute the dried cranberries with other dried fruit, such as raisins, mulberries, or dried blueberries. Swap the apple juice for nut milk (e.g. Almond Milk on page 146) or Homemade Yogurt (page 151).

★ Optional extras
Add chopped fresh seasonal fruit. Sweeten with a little stevia if desired.

BASIC OIL-FREE GRANOLA

When you don't have much time in the morning but want to eat something
filling and nourishing, granola with plant-based milk, fruit, or yogurt is the answer.
To provide maximum energy with minimum calories use apple sauce, mashed ripe
banana, or other fruit purées instead of oil. You can easily experiment with your own
favorite ingredients to make a perfect granola mix.

Makes 8 servings

☆	☆	☆	☆	☆	☆	☆
3 cups rolled grains (e.g. oats, rye, buckwheat, quinoa, or a mixture of the above)	⅓ cup chopped nuts or seeds (e.g. almonds, walnuts, pistachios, sunflower, or pumpkin seeds or coconut flakes)	1 teaspoon ground cinnamon and/or ½ teaspoon vanilla powder/ extract (optional)	5 tablespoons brown rice syrup or maple syrup	½ cup apple purée or mashed banana	1 cup dried fruit (e.g. raisins, mulberries, or goji berries)	Dried flower petals, such as rose (optional)

Preheat the oven to 300°F and line a baking sheet with parchment paper.

Mix the grains, nuts, or seeds and cinnamon and/or vanilla (if using) in a large bowl
with a pinch of salt. Add the brown rice syrup or maple syrup and the apple purée or
mashed banana and mix until well combined. Spread the mixture out evenly on the
baking sheet and bake in the oven for 20 minutes.

Remove the tray from the oven and gently fold and mix the granola to avoid getting
big clumps. Bake for another 20 minutes, watching closely and mixing again, if
needed, until golden brown. Remove from the oven and leave to cool and become
crisp.

When cooled completely, mix in the dried fruit and dried flower petals (if using).
Store in an airtight container for up to 1 month.

BREAKFAST BARS

This is the ideal on-the-go breakfast for those mornings when you've pressed the snooze button on your alarm too many times! My little daughter loves one of these for her breakfast, but I reserve them for a special treat rather than for every day. Full of flavor and goodness, they also make a great midday snack.

Makes 24 bars

☆	☆	☆	☆	☆	☆	☆
1½ cups rolled oats	4 cups puffed quinoa	¾ cup dried cranberries (or other dried fruit)	⅓ cup raw shelled pistachios (or other nuts or seeds)	1 cup nut butter (e.g. almond or tahini)	½ cup rice syrup (or maple syrup)	2 teaspoons ground cinnamon

Line a baking sheet with parchment paper.

Toast the oats in a pan over medium heat, stirring frequently, for about 5 minutes. Transfer to a bowl, add the quinoa, cranberries, and pistachios and mix together.

Place the nut butter, rice syrup, and cinnamon in a pan with a pinch of salt and heat over low heat, stirring well to prevent sticking or burning, until the mixture is a smooth liquid, about 1½ minutes.

Pour the nutty syrup over the dried ingredients and stir until evenly mixed. Pour the mixture onto the prepared baking sheet and spread out to create an even layer, pressing down carefully to ensure that the bars will hold together. Place in the freezer for at least 30 minutes.

Remove from the freezer and cut into bars. Store in the fridge for 2 weeks or in the freezer for 3 months.

★ Variation
Try adding 2 teaspoons chopped fresh rosemary with the other dry ingredients.

MILLET PORRIDGE WITH ORANGE-ROASTED RHUBARB

Millet is a tiny, round ancient grain that is gluten-free. Depending on how much liquid you add and how much you stir it, it can be cooked into a creamy mash or kept so it has a drier texture, similar to couscous. It tastes slightly nutty and marries perfectly with roasted rhubarb, a pairing I was inspired to try by Susann Probst and Yannic Schon from @krautkopf. It's ideal for chilly mornings when you long for something filling and delicious. It's not overly sweet, so add some maple syrup or other sweetener to serve if you like.

Serves 2

☆	☆	☆	☆	☆	☆
3½ cups millet, rinsed and drained	5–6 stalks rhubarb, cut into 1.5 to 2-inch batons	Zest and juice of 1 orange	3 tablespoons brown rice syrup or maple syrup	4 cups Almond Milk (page 146)	¼ cup almonds, roughly chopped

If possible, soak the millet overnight then rinse and drain.

Preheat the oven to 350°F.

Mix the rhubarb with the orange zest and juice, syrup, and a grinding of black pepper in a bowl, then transfer to a baking dish. Cover with foil or dampened parchment paper and cook for 15 minutes.

Remove the foil or paper and cook for an additional 5 to 10 minutes until the rhubarb is tender but still holds its shape.

In the meantime, cook the porridge. Place the millet and almond milk in a pot over medium heat and bring to a boil, stirring regularly. Reduce the temperature to low to prevent it from burning and cook for about 25 minutes (or 12 to 13 minutes if the millet was soaked overnight), continuing to stir regularly, until it is creamy and smooth.

Spoon some porridge into a bowl and add a couple of tablespoons of the rhubarb compote and its juices. Top with some chopped almonds.

★ Tips
Any leftover rhubarb compote is also very good with a little plant-based yogurt and some granola, or with pancakes.

JAPANESE-STYLE PORRIDGE

In summer, I really like my breakfasts sweet and fresh – smoothies or muesli with lots of fresh fruit – but come winter, my body craves warmer, more savory dishes. As a child I was raised on a macrobiotic diet, so I often ate miso soup in the morning. This gave me the idea of adding miso to my regular porridge. With the addition of gomashio, which gives this dish an extra Japanese touch, the result is a truly satisfying way to start the day.

Serves 2

☆	☆	☆	☆	☆	☆
1¼ cups barley flakes (or rye, quinoa flakes or rolled oats)	¾ cup sesame seeds (ideally a mix of brown and black)	1 ripe avocado	1 tablespoon mild miso (e.g. shiro miso) diluted in 3 tablespoons water	A handful of your favorite sprout (such as radish sprouts or pea sprouts)	2 scallions, chopped

To make the porridge, put the barley flakes (or other grain) into a pot with 2 cups water and bring to a boil. Reduce the heat to low and cook for 15 minutes until soft.

Meanwhile, make your sesame sprinkle or gomashio. Wash the sesame seeds and drain in a fine-mesh strainer. Pour into a cast-iron (or heavy-bottomed) pan or skillet and dry-fry over a medium heat, stirring often, for 5 to 8 minutes until fragrant and lightly golden. (Keep an eye on them as they burn easily.) Leave to cool, then grind together with 2 teaspoons salt, either using a mortar and pestle or a food-processor.

Just before the porridge is ready, cut the avocado in half and remove the pit, then peel and slice. When ready, remove the porridge from the heat and stir in the miso.

Divide the porridge between two bowls and top with the avocado, sprouts, scallions, and a good sprinkle of the gomashio.

★ Tip
Try the leftover gomashio on salads, steamed vegetables, or any grain dishes.

VEGAN KUKU SABZI

Kuku (pronounced koo-koo) is a savory Iranian omelet. The word "sabzi" refers to the large amount of herbs used, which make this a beautifully green and very tasty way to start to the day. Chickpea flour is a perfect egg substitute and this amount makes four individual "omelets."

Serves 4

☆	☆	☆	☆	☆	☆	☆
¾ cup chickpea flour	Bunch of fresh parsley, chopped	Bunch of fresh cilantro, chopped	½ bunch of fresh dill, chopped	4 scallions, chopped	¾ cup chopped walnuts	Nut-based yogurt or hot sauce, to serve

Mix the chickpea flour with ⅔ cup water in a bowl and stir until smooth and free of lumps. Stir in the chopped herbs, scallions, walnuts, and ¼ teaspoon salt.

Heat a nonstick skillet over high heat (adding a little olive oil or coconut oil if necessary). Spoon in a quarter of the batter, swirl around the skillet to spread evenly, and cook for about 2 minutes. When the top is dry, carefully flip it over and cook the other side for 2 minutes.

Transfer the "omelet" to a plate and cover with a piece of foil to keep it warm while you cook the other three "omelets." Serve with yogurt or hot sauce such as Ajvar (page 163).

SAVORY EGGLESS MUFFINS

These savory treats are perfect for brunch, a packed lunch, or picnic. They are so easy to make: you simply flavor the muffins with whatever leftover ingredients you have and then the oven does almost all the rest of the work for you. The ones here are made with oyster mushrooms and greens, but you can add all sorts of cooked vegetables, such as tomatoes, beans, and broccoli.

Makes 9

☆	☆	☆	☆	☆	☆
14 oz. silken tofu, drained	⅓ cup chickpea flour	¼ teaspoon ground turmeric (optional, for color)	1 medium red onion, chopped	9 oz. mushrooms (e.g. oyster mushrooms), roughly chopped	A handful of greens (e.g. spinach or kale)

Preheat the oven to 350°F.

Mix the silken tofu, chickpea flour, turmeric, and ¼ teaspoon salt in a blender until you have a smooth batter.

Heat 2 tablespoons of water in a skillet over medium heat, then add the onion and cook until golden brown, adding a little more water if necessary to prevent burning. Add the mushrooms and fry until cooked, then add the greens and cook until wilted. Season with salt and pepper and let sit.

Stir the cooked mushroom and greens into the batter. Pour the batter into nonstick or silicone muffin molds and bake for 25 minutes in the oven until lighlty browned.

Leave to cool for 10 minutes before eating. You can also eat your muffins chilled. They will last in the fridge for 3 to 4 days.

BREAD "LASAGNA" WITH ALMOND CUSTARD

In France, where I live for part of the year, most bread has to be eaten fresh as it contains no additives, so I always have leftovers. There are various traditional and delicious ways to use stale bread, including France's "pain perdu" and Britain's bread pudding. This bread "lasagna" makes a lovely breakfast – perfect for a lazy weekend morning.

Serves 4 to 6

☆	☆	☆	☆	☆	☆	☆
6 slices of stale wholegrain bread (I like to use spelt)	3¼ cups Almond Milk (page 146)	½ cup brown rice syrup or maple syrup	1 teaspoon ground cinnamon or ground cardamom	1 teaspoon vanilla powder or vanilla extract	3 tablespoons arrowroot or cornstarch mixed with 7 tablespoons water	7½ cups mixed berries (or slices of orange and pear)

Preheat the oven to 350°F.

Cut the bread into small pieces to fit in two layers in a ceramic baking dish approx. 7 x 11 x 2 inches).

Prepare the custard by heating the almond milk with the brown rice syrup (or maple syrup), cinnamon or cardamom, and the vanilla in a pot. Bring it to a boil, then reduce the heat and add the dissolved arrowroot or cornstarch mixture. Stir until thickened, then remove from the heat.

Pour 1 cup of the custard into the baking dish to coat the bottom, then top with half of the bread pieces. Pour another 1 cup of the custard over the bread and spread half the fruit on top of it. Repeat the bread layer, pour over the remaining custard and bake in the oven for 20 to 25 minutes.

The "lasagna" is ready when the fruit is bubbling and the top of the bread is golden. Remove from the oven, scatter with the remaining fresh fruit and serve.

★ Optional extras
You can serve this sweet "lasagna" with Homemade Yogurt (page 151) or Sweet Cashew Cream (page 150).

CHIA JAM

My neighbors regularly present me with bucketloads of fruit picked from their trees, which are perfect for jam. Adding chia seeds is not only healthy, but delicious too. Try it on toast, pancakes, or with yogurt. For a smoother consistency, mash the fruit with a fork after simmering.

APRICOT, ALMOND & VANILLA

Makes one pint jar

☆	☆	☆	☆	☆	☆
2½ cups apricots, pitted	Juice of ½ lemon	¼ cup brown rice syrup or maple syrup	Seeds of ½ vanilla pod	2 to 3 tablespoons chia seeds	¾ cup blanched almonds

Roughly chop the apricots, then add to a pot with the lemon juice, syrup, vanilla, and 4 tablespoons of water. Bring to a gentle boil then simmer for 5 to 8 minutes.

Remove from the heat and stir in 2½ tablespoons of chia seeds and the almonds, roughly chopped. The chia seeds will expand, so leave for 5 minutes to thicken. If you prefer a thicker consistency, add more chia seeds, a teaspoonful at a time.

Once cooled, transfer the jam to a sterilized lidded glass jar and store in the fridge. It will keep for 2 weeks after opening. Otherwise, freeze for up to 3 months.

BLACKBERRY, PLUM & BLACK PEPPER

Makes one pint jar

☆	☆	☆	☆	☆
1¾ cups blackberries	1½ cups plums, pitted and chopped	Juice of ½ lemon	¼ cup maple syrup (or to taste)	2 to 3 tablespoons chia seeds

Combine the blackberries, plums, lemon juice, and maple syrup with 2 tablespoons of water and a good grind of black pepper. Simmer over a low heat for 5 to 8 minutes.

Turn off the heat and add 2½ tablespoons of chia seeds. Leave to thicken for 5 to 10 minutes, then add more chia seeds, if needed, to reach the consistency you want.

Once cooled, transfer the jam to a sterilized lidded glass jar and store in the fridge.

START

OATMEAL & BANANA CUPS

On mornings when you don't need to rush and you feel like making something extra special for breakfast, these baked oat cups are perfect. They are a true feast for the eyes and tastebuds and not too complicated to make either. Dessert for breakfast is maybe a better way to describe them!

Makes 10 cups

☆	☆	☆	☆	☆	☆
2 medium bananas, chopped	4 Medjool dates, pitted	1 teaspoon vanilla extract	2½ cups finely rolled oats	1¼ cups Homemade Yogurt (page 151)	Fresh fruit— kiwi, berries, apricots, mango, passionfruit

Preheat the oven to 350°F. Peel and chop your fruit, if necessary.

Blend the banana, Medjool dates, and vanilla together with a pinch of salt in a blender. Pour into a large bowl, add the oats, and stir together until combined.

Spoon 1½ tablespoons of the oat mixture into a nonstick or silicone muffin mold, using your thumb to create a little nest in the center. Repeat until you have used up all the mixture (you should have enough to make 10 cups).

Bake in the oven for 18 to 20 minutes until golden brown.

Remove from the oven and leave to cool and become crisp. Spoon 1 to 1½ tablespoons yogurt into each "cup" and top with the prepared fruit.

TOFU SCRAMBLE

If you're craving something hearty and savory for breakfast, tofu scramble fits the bill perfectly and takes mere minutes to make. I don't usually use meat or dairy replacers, but once in a while organic non-GMO tofu can be a fun ingredient to play around with. This recipe uses black salt or "kala namak," a highly sulphuric salt that comes from India and gives this scramble a realistic eggy smell and taste.

Serves 2

☆	☆	☆	☆	☆	☆
9 oz. block of firm tofu	1 small onion, finely chopped	⅔ cup watercress or other fresh greens (e.g. spinach or kale—if using kale, chop it into smaller pieces so it cooks evenly)	Pinch of turmeric	Pinch of chili powder or freshly ground black pepper	Pinch of black salt or kala namak

Rinse and drain the tofu, then wrap it in some paper towels to absorb excess water.

Place the onions in a nonstick ceramic pan with a splash of water and cook over medium heat until soft and golden (about 3 to 4 minutes). Add a splash more water if needed to prevent them from sticking. Reduce the heat to low.

Meanwhile, crumble the tofu in a bowl using a fork, or pulse in a food-processor until evenly chopped.

Add the tofu to the onions together with the greens, turmeric, chili powder, or black pepper and black salt. Add 3 to 4 tablespoons of water, increase the heat to medium and cook until the greens are wilted. Taste and add some more black salt and pepper, if needed, then serve.

★ Serving suggestion
Serve with toast, leftover grains, or potatoes and, if you want to give it a bit of a kick, a bit of chili sauce, such as the Asian Sweet and Spicy Sauce on page 163.

BREAKFAST TACO

Nuts are often used as a substitute for meat, particularly in a raw food diet, as when seasoned, they have a similar flavor. If you have time, leave the nuts overnight so that they thoroughly soak up all up the flavors. Here are two versions of "nut meat": one with North African flavors, the other with Mexican.

Serves 4

☆	☆	☆	☆	☆	☆
2 medium onions, chopped	1½ cups raw walnuts, soaked for at least 2 hours	2½ oz. sun-dried tomatoes, soaked in hot water for at least 1 hour (or ready-soaked in a jar)	3 teaspoons ras el hanout	Steamed greens, to serve	Lemon Tahini dressing (page 160), to serve

Fry the onions in a skillet with a splash of water or oil until golden and translucent, about 5 minutes.

Drain the walnuts and tomatoes. Roughly chop the tomatoes then transfer both to a food-processor with the onions and ras el hanout. Pulse until crumbly, but don't overdo it or you will end up with "butter". Taste and add salt if necessary.

Either gently warm the "meat" in a pan ove a medium heat, or serve at room temperature with steamed greens and Lemon Tahini dressing.

★ **Variations**
For a Mexican version, swap the ras el hanout for a Mexican spice mix and serve the "meat" in a red cabbage leaf or tortilla with avocado and some iceberg lettuce. If you feel brave enough, add some jalapeño peppers.

★ **Optional extras**
1 teaspoon of granulated garlic can be added when the "meat" is pulsed together, if you like. When they're in season, I like to serve with some beautiful tomatoes.

☆
START

★
FRESH

☆
FAST

☆
NOURISH

☆
GATHER

☆
SWEET

☆
BASIC

BEET TZATZIKI

Beet juice is such a gorgeous color that I would like to bottle it for a lipstick!
The earthy flavor is not everyone's favorite, but this creamy recipe makes for a
delicious starter.

Serves 4 to 6

☆	☆	☆	☆	☆
1 lb. medium raw (or boiled) beets, scrubbed	¾ cup plant-based yogurt	2 garlic cloves, finely chopped	1 teaspoon orange or lemon zest	3 tablespoons chopped fresh mint

Place the beets in a pot, cover with water, then cook covered for about 40 to 45
minutes. They are done when you can easily insert a knife through them.

Leave to cool completely, then grate into a large bowl.

Mix the grated beets with the yogurt, garlic, orange or lemon zest, and
½ teaspoon sea salt. Scatter with the chopped fresh mint to serve.

SUNFLOWER PÂTÉ

Fill small peppers with this pâté for a great appetizer, or serve it as a dip with raw
veggies. You could also spread it on a nori sheet as a rice alternative in sushi.

Makes about 2 cups pâté

☆	☆	☆	☆	☆	☆	☆
1 cup sunflower seeds, soaked overnight and drained	2 celery stalks, chopped	2 garlic cloves, crushed	3 teaspoons dried oregano	1 tablespoon white miso	Juice of 1 lemon	1 bunch of chives (about ¼ cup), finely chopped

Put all the ingredients, except the chives, in a food-processor and blend until
smooth. Add salt and pepper to taste, then transfer to a bowl and stir in the chives.

Keep chilled in the fridge until ready to serve.

SPRING PEA SOUP WITH ROASTED RADISHES

I first made pea soup when I unexpectedly had to cook for guests with only a big bag of peas and a few leftovers at hand. My guests were astounded that I'd managed to concoct such a delicious and healthy-looking soup from so little. This Spring variation includes roasted radishes and is a delicious way to celebrate the new arrival of fresh, seasonal produce – a nice prelude to warmer times.

Serves 4

☆	☆	☆	☆	☆	☆	☆
7 oz. radishes, quartered	4 cups vegetable stock (page 155) or water	1 bunch of scallions, chopped	1 lb. 5 oz. frozen peas	6 oz. spinach leaves, shredded (or a mix of leaves, e.g. spinach, sorrel, wild nettle)	A swirl of Savory Cashew Cream (page 150, to serve (optional)	Chopped fresh chervil, to serve (optional)

Preheat the oven to 350°F and line a baking sheet with parchment paper.

Toss the radishes in a bowl with a splash of stock or water and a pinch of salt and pepper. Spread them out on the prepared baking sheet and bake for 15 to 20 minutes, turning them every 5 minutes. They should be tender with a firm center and have a lovely pink color when done.

Meanwhile, make the soup. Put the scallions, reserving 3 tablespoons, into a pot with a splash of water and cook over medium heat for 5 to 10 minutes to soften. Add the remaining water or vegetable stock and bring to a boil. Add the peas, spinach leaves, 1½ teaspoons salt and a good pinch of pepper. Lower the heat and simmer for an additional 2 to 3 minutes, then remove the pot from the heat and mix the soup using an immersion blender or a blender. Taste and add more seasoning if needed.

Serve scattered with the roasted radishes, reserved chopped scallions, chervil, and, if you like, some Savory Cashew Cream.

CORN SOUP WITH GREEN TOMATO SALSA

When corn is widely available, my daughter, given her way, will eat corn on the cob almost every day. For some variety, I make this soup with a green tomato salsa, which gives a perfect little kick. Make sure you choose organic corn: nowadays, nonorganic corn is usually heavily sprayed, genetically modified, and extensively hybridized.

Serves 4

☆	☆	☆	☆	☆	☆	☆
1 lb. corn from about 3 to 4 corn cobs (depending on size)	3 scallions, finely chopped, green and white parts separated	2 garlic cloves, crushed	1 avocado, not too ripe	3 medium green tomatoes, quartered, deseeded, and diced	1 fresh jalapeño pepper or other green chile, finely chopped	Juice of ½ lime

Remove the husks and silks from the corn cobs. Use a knife to remove the kernels and let sit.

Heat a pot over medium heat and add the whites of the scallions and a splash of water. Cook until transparent, adding a little more water if needed. Add the garlic, stir, and cook for an additional minute, then add the corn kernels and 3 cups water. Bring to a boil with the lid on, then reduce the heat and leave to simmer for 8 to 10 minutes, until the corn is soft.

Blend the soup using an immersion blender until silky smooth. Season with salt and pepper to taste, then return to the pan and place over a low heat to keep warm.

Peel and remove the pit from the avocado and finely dice the flesh. Put it in a small bowl and mix in the chopped scallion greens, tomato, jalapeño (to taste), lime juice, and some salt. Pour the soup into serving bowls and float two tablespoons of the salsa on top of each.

★ Tips

If you can't find green tomatoes, use regular tomatoes or 10 to 12 tomatillos instead. You could also replace the tomatoes with ½ a cucumber, deseeded and finely chopped. If you can't find fresh jalapeño peppers, you can use chopped jalapeño from a jar. You will need 1 to 2 tablespoons, depending on how hot you like it.

TEMPEH CRUMBLE IN LETTUCE CUPS

Tempeh is an Indonesian fermented soybean product that is widely used as a meat substitute. It often forms part of the Dutch–Indonesian rijsttafel (literally "rice table") – a meal consisting of a large number of small Indonesian dishes. Although the individual dishes are all Indonesian, the meal as a whole was invented by Dutch colonialists so they could enjoy a variety of Indonesian dishes at the same time.

Serves 4 to 6 as an appetizer

☆	☆	☆	☆	☆	☆
10 oz. tempeh, finely chopped or roughly grated	1 thumb-sized piece of fresh ginger, finely grated	6 tablespoons tamari or nama shoyu	1 tablespoon coconut syrup or coconut sugar	2 teaspoons brown rice vinegar or lemon juice	12 little gem lettuce leaves

Put the tempeh in a nonstick ceramic pan with a splash of water and cook for 4 to 5 minutes over medium–high heat, stirring frequently.

Meanwhile, in a small bowl, mix the ginger, tamari or nama shoyu, coconut syrup or sugar, and rice vinegar or lemon juice together with 6 tablespoons of water. Pour this mixture over the tempeh and stir. Cook for an additional 3 to 4 minutes, stirring frequently, then cool for 2 minutes.

Arrange the salad leaves on a plate and top with the tempeh and any additions of your choice (see below).

★ Optional extras
These lettuce cups are delicious served with some hot sauce (e.g. the Asian Sweet and Spicy Sauce on page 163) or finely chopped fresh chiles. They are also great combined with pickled or fresh cucumber, sesame seeds, and finely sliced scallions.

FENNEL, WATERCRESS, ORANGE & AVOCADO SALAD

Great-looking salads are my favorite starters. This one is light, delicious, and craveable, especially on a hot day, and is a wonderful dish to serve alfresco in the summer sun.

Serves 4

☆	☆	☆	☆	☆
2 fennel bulbs, trimmed (fronds reserved)	2 oranges	2 firm avocados	1 teaspoon coriander seeds	6 oz. watercress, thick stalks removed

Thinly slice the fennel using a mandoline, if you have one. Juice half of one of the oranges, then mix the juice with a pinch of salt, some pepper, and the thinly sliced fennel. Leave to marinate for 5 to 10 minutes.

Cut each avocado in half and remove the pit. Remove the flesh using a tablespoon and cut each half lengthways into three slices. Place a grill pan over medium–high heat and griddle the avocado slices for 3 minutes, gently flipping them over halfway. Let sit.

Meanwhile, heat a skillet over low heat and dry-fry the coriander seeds for 1 minute. Remove the seeds from the skillet and crush in a mortar.

Skin the remaining orange by cutting away the peel and the white membrane, then slice into segments or into large rounds.

Drain the fennel and reserve the juice. Mix the latter with 2 tablespoons extra virgin olive oil to make the dressing. Taste and add more salt or pepper if needed.

Assemble by layering the watercress first, then the fennel, oranges, and grilled avocado. Top with the crushed coriander seeds and reserved fennel fronds, then drizzle the dressing over the salad. Serve immediately.

TOMATO, TARRAGON, NECTARINE & HORSERADISH SALAD

This salad is made from summer's finest produce and is bursting with flavor. Savory Cashew Cream (page 150) is used as a base for the dressing, with some added horseradish to give it an extra punch. If you don't have time to make the Cashew Cream, replace it with silken tofu blended with a tablespoon of lemon juice and some salt, or with plant-based yogurt.

Serves 4

☆	☆	☆	☆	☆	☆	☆
4 tomatoes (a mixture of colors, if available), sliced into wedges	4 nectarines, sliced into wedges	½ cucumber, deseeded and sliced into wedges	2 teaspoons white balsamic vinegar	1 batch Savory Cashew Cream (page 150)	1 teaspoon grated horseradish	1 bunch of tarragon, leaves torn

In a large bowl, toss the tomatoes, nectarines, and cucumber together with the balsamic vinegar and add a pinch of salt and pepper.

In a small bowl, stir together the cashew cream and horseradish with a pinch of salt and pepper.

Put some dollops of cream on a large plate (or individual ones), arrange the salad nicely on top, and scatter the torn tarragon leaves on top.

ZUCCHINI NOODLE SALAD

In summer, I have the luxury of wandering through my garden, looking for what is in season to use for dinner. Young, firm zucchini are delicious when cut into noodles (or "zoodles"). The vegan "Parmesan" brings a salty balance to this recipe and can be used in many other dishes, for example with pasta. So feel free to double or triple the amount you make, because it never lasts long!

Serves 2 as a main, 4 as a starter

☆	☆	☆	☆	☆	☆	☆
¼ cup pine nuts	½ teaspoon garlic powder (optional)	3 tablespoons nutritional yeast	2 medium zucchini, trimmed	1 cup raspberries	Leaves from 4 to 5 sprigs of thyme	6 oz. mixed young salad leaves

Start by making the pine nut "Parmesan." In a food-processor, combine the pine nuts, garlic powder, if using, and yeast with ½ teaspoon of sea salt and pulse until a grated Parmesan-like consistency is formed. Store in an airtight container.

Slice the zucchini into long thin strips using a mandoline, spiralizer, or a potato peeler.

To make the dressing, mash ⅓ cup of the raspberries with 5 tablespoons extra virgin olive oil. Add the thyme leaves, a pinch of sea salt, and freshly ground black pepper.

Toss the salad leaves and the zucchini noodles with the dressing. Sprinkle with the remaining raspberries and 4 to 5 tablespoons of pine nut "Parmesan".

★ Variation
For a more budget-friendly nut "Parmesan," use equal parts of cashews and sunflower seeds.

RADICCHIO & GRILLED FIG SALAD WITH NUT BALLS

Radicchio is a gorgeous red salad leaf with quite a bitter taste, so it needs some balance from salty, sweet flavours and creamy tones. The ingredients in this salad provide just that, making it a perfect and very addictive autumn dish.

Serves 4

☆	☆	☆	☆	☆	☆	☆
¾ cup Almond Curd (page 147) or vegan "cream cheese"	1 garlic clove, finely chopped	¾ cup walnuts, very finely chopped	2 tablespoons white balsamic vinegar	8 ripe figs, halved	1 head of radicchio, shredded	3 oz. rocket

Put the Almond Curd or cream cheese in a bowl and season well with garlic, salt, and a good amount of freshly ground black pepper. Spread the finely chopped walnuts out on a plate.

With slightly damp hands, take a teaspoon of the mixture and form a little ball, then roll it in the chopped walnuts. Repeat until all the mixture is used, then let sit. You can make the balls ahead of time and store them in the fridge, if you wish.

In a small bowl, mix together the white balsamic vinegar and 5 tablespoons of olive oil and season with salt and pepper. Let sit.

Preheat a grill pan over high heat. Lightly brush the halved figs with a little oil. When the grill pan is hot, place the fig halves on it, cut-side down. After 30 seconds, carefully lift the first fig you put in the pan. If there are grill marks on it, turn it over; if not, wait a bit longer. After all are turned and cooked, remove them from the pan, using tongs, and let sit.

To serve, layer the radicchio and arugula, place the almond and walnut balls and roasted figs on top and spoon over a little dressing.

★ Variation

If you want to make this salad oil-free, brush the figs with a little maple syrup instead of oil and omit the oil from the dressing.

FAVA BEAN SALAD WITH FREEKEH

Salads are perfect when it's hot and you want a light meal, but they can be so much more than just leaves. Adding beans or grains can turn it into a substantial, filling meal. This dish uses freekeh – roasted young green wheat that has its origin in the Middle East. It has a beautiful nutty taste and looks a bit like bulgur. This recipe is the perfect substitute for a regular couscous salad.

Serves 2 as a main or 4 as a starter

☆	☆	☆	☆	☆	☆	☆
3½ oz. freekeh (if you can't find it, use bulgur instead)	2½ cups shelled fava beans (about 10 cups) fresh unshelled fava beans)	2 lemons	1 large bunch of fresh mint, leaves chopped	6 oz. salad leaves (arugula, baby spinach, or lamb's lettuce)	¾ cup almonds, chopped	Juice of ½ lime

Cook the freekeh according to the package instructions. Drain, if necessary, then put it into a large bowl, and leave to cool slightly.

Meanwhile, bring 4 cups of water to a boil in a pot. (Don't salt the water as salt will toughen the beans.) Put the beans in the boiling water and simmer for 5 to 7 minutes (very small ones will need only 3 to 4 minutes). Drain the beans and rinse them with cold water. Mix with the freekeh, season with salt and let sit.

Halve the lemons and cook them on a grill pan (or a normal nonstick ceramic one) for 4 to 5 minutes.

Combine the freekeh and fava beans with the mint, salad leaves, and chopped almonds. Season with salt and pepper if needed and drizzle with 3 to 4 tablespoons of olive oil. Serve with the salad and a wedge of lemon to squeeze over it.

★ Variations
As an alternative to olive oil, dress with the Lemon Tahini Dressing on page 160.
To make this salad gluten free, replace the freekeh with cooked quinoa.

STUFFED ZUCCHINI FLOWERS

Growing vegetables is fun and zucchini always do well – when summer is
in full swing the plants produce more than I can eat, as well as beautiful fresh
edible flowers. You can also get them at farmers' markets, or ask at your local
grocer's. The flowers are often stuffed and deep-fried but, in my opinion, this
wastes their delicate flavor. I prefer them raw and packed with a delicious creamy
filling. This starter will certainly impress your guests!

Makes 8

☆	☆	☆	☆	☆
¾ cup Almond Curd (page 147) or vegan "cream cheese"	2 oz. olives, pitted and chopped	8 sun-dried tomatoes, rehydrated in some hot water for 15 to 20 minutes, or from a jar, chopped	3 tablespoons chopped or torn basil leaves	8 zucchini flowers

Mix the Almond Curd in a bowl with the chopped olives, sun-dried tomatoes, basil,
and season with salt and pepper to taste.

Gently open a zucchini flower and stuff with 2 to 3 teaspoons of the filling. With clean
hands, carefully close the flower. Repeat with the remaining flowers and stuffing.
Serve immediately.

★ Variations
To enojy warm, bake the stuffed flowers in a preheated oven at 350°F for 15 minutes.

FRENCH-STYLE SHIITAKE "SNAILS"

The idea for these shiitake "snails" came to me when I was wandering in a charity shop and my eye was caught by a plate, the sort used to serve escargots à la bourguignonne (snails with parsley, garlic, and butter). I wondered if I could "veganize" this classic French meal by using shiitake mushrooms, which have a similarly chewy texture. If you cut around the stem and remove it, then make a small cut in the cap from the outside to the middle, the mushroom unfurls and looks like a long curly "snail."

Serves 4 as an appetizer

☆	☆	☆	☆	☆
1 lb. 5 oz. shiitake mushrooms	1 shallot or 1 small onion, finely diced	4 to 6 garlic cloves, finely chopped	1 bunch of parsley, chopped	2 teaspoons tamari or nama shoyu

Cut around the stem of each mushroom, then make a small cut in the cap toward the middle. Discard the stem. You now have a shiitake "snail." Repeat the process until all are done.

Cook the onions in a pan with a splash of water until soft, about 5 minutes.

Add the "snails" to the pan with a pinch of salt. Once the mushrooms have released some moisture, add the garlic and most of the parsley (reserving some for garnish). Keep stirring and, if needed, add a small amount of water. Sauté for 4 to 5 minutes, then add the tamari or nama shoyu and cook for an additional 2 minutes.

Sprinkle with the reserved parsley and serve with some soda bread if you wish.

SMOKED CARROT LAX BITES

I think it's great fun to substitute familiar foods with plant-based versions. My Carrot Lax are inspired by the Scandinavian Gravad Lax, a cured salmon dish. This looks and tastes almost the same as the real deal. It's endlessly versatile and has a wonderful salty and smoky flavor. The latter comes from liquid smoke, an ingredient you can find online and in vegan shops. You can also use smoked paprika, although the taste won't be quite the same. The lax takes two or three days, so you'll need to practice a little patience.

Serves 4

☆	☆	☆	☆	☆	☆	☆
1 lb. unpeeled carrots	1 teaspoon liquid smoke or smoked paprika	2 tablespoons mirin (Japanese cooking wine)	1 quantity Savory Cashew Cream (page 150) or vegan "cream cheese"	2 red onions, sliced into thin half moons	1 jar capers in brine	4 tablespoons chopped fresh dill

Preheat the oven to 350°F.

Wrap the carrots in foil and bake for 45 to 60 minutes until cooked but still al dente.

Carefully remove the peel and slice the carrots as thin as you can, either on the diagonal or in long strips. Place the slices in a bowl and add the liquid smoke, mirin, lemon juice, and ½ teaspoon salt. Stir to coat well.

Place the carrots in a container, cover with a lid or foil, and refrigerate for 2 to 3 days before serving, to allow the flavors to develop.

Serve with a small amount of Savory Cashew Cream, some thin strips of red onion, and a couple of capers. Grind some black pepper on top and sprinkle with fresh dill.

★ Serving suggestion
Serve with seeded crackers of your choice. The Carrot Lax also works great in pastas, quiches, or salads.

SUMMER ROLLS

These summer rolls are a light way to start any meal, or perfect as a simple lunch. Once you start rolling, they're pretty easy – and fun – to make!

Makes 8

☆	☆	☆	☆	☆	☆	☆
8 round rice paper wrappers	1 bunch of fresh mint	1 bunch of fresh (Thai) basil	1 cucumber, deseeded and cut into strips	1 mango, peeled, pit removed and cut into strips	1 avocado, peeled, pit removed and cut into strips	2 red peppers, deseeded and cut into strips

Pour some lukewarm water into a heatproof bowl large enough for the wrappers to fit in without folding. Dip a wrapper in the water and hold for 5 to 10 seconds until it is soft and pliable.

Lay the wrapper on a clean, flat surface and layer some of each of the remaining ingredients in the center of your wrapper. Fold in the left and right side and the part that is closest to you over the filling. Roll gently but tightly so the roll keeps its shape. Place under a damp cloth and repeat with the remaining wrappers, then serve immediately.

★ Optional extras
These rolls are delicious on their own, but you can serve them with Asian Sweet and Spicy Sauce (page 163), tamari or Peanut Sauce (page 65), if you wish.
To make these rolls more substantial, try adding sprouts, smoked tofu, and/or soaked mung bean noodles.

☆ START ☆ FRESH ★ **FAST** ☆ NOURISH ☆ GATHER ☆ SWEET ☆ BASIC

PASTA WITH TAPENADE & GRILLED CHERRY TOMATOES

One of my earliest memories is looking forward to the treat of a big green olive at the local market with my mom, and I've loved them ever since. Storebought olive tapenade is often made with anchovies, so I make my own vegan version. Use the best quality pitted olives to ensure a superior taste – either black ones, such as Kalamata or Nyons (from the South of France), or green depending on your preference. Tapenade mixed with pasta and oven-roasted tomatoes makes my perfect 15-minute meal.

Serves 4 to 6

☆	☆	☆	☆	☆	☆	☆
1 lb. cherry tomatoes	2 teaspoons (white) balsamic vinegar	1 lb. pasta	5 oz. pitted olives, black or green	3 oz. sun-dried tomatoes	2 garlic cloves, roughly chopped	2 oz. arugula or parsley, chopped

Preheat the oven to 425°F.

Place the cherry tomatoes in a baking pan, drizzle over the balsamic vinegar, and season with salt and pepper. Shake to coat the tomatoes place in the oven for 12 to 15 minutes.

Fill a large pan with water, place on medium to high heat, and bring to a boil. Cook the pasta according to the package instructions. When done, drain, reserving 3 tablespoons of the cooking liquid.

Meanwhile, , put the olives, sun-dried tomatoes, garlic, and arugula or parsley in a food-processor, and pulse chop until well combined. This will keep for 5 to 6 days in the fridge.

Stir ¾ cup of the tapenade with the pasta and the reserved cooking liquid to loosen the mixture. Add a little more tapenade to taste. Serve with the cherry tomatoes on top.

★ Tip
I like to use wholegrain, sprouted, or gluten-free pasta, or pasta made from beans.

SWEET POTATO FRIES WITH SPICY GUACAMOLE

In the Netherlands there are chip shops (we call them "snackbars") around every corner. The chips are fried twice in oil, which, for me, is two reasons not to eat them: too much fat and too unhealthy. But, I do enjoy eating fast food if I do it my own way. Food prepared quickly can be delicious and healthy, and these oven-baked sweet potato chips will be done in less time than it takes to get to your local takeout joint and back again. Pairing fries with a good guacamole makes an interesting change to the classic mayonnaise.

Serves 4

☆	☆	☆	☆	☆
3 lbs. 5 oz. sweet potatoes, unpeeled, cut into chips	3 ripe avocados	Juice of 1 lime	1 to 2 garlic cloves, finely chopped	½–1 fresh jalapeño pepper, deseeded and finely chopped

Preheat the oven to 425°F (fan assisted if possible) and line a baking sheet with parchment paper.

Place a pot of water over high heat and bring to a boil. Add the sweet potato fries and cook for 2 minutes, then drain.

Lay the sweet potatoes on the baking sheet, season with salt and pepper, and bake for 20 to 25 minutes, shaking from time to time. They are done when they are golden brown on the outside and soft on the inside.

Meanwhile, make the guacamole by removing the skin and pits from the avocados. Mash the flesh in a bowl with a fork (or use a food-processor). Mix in the lime juice, garlic, jalapeño pepper, and a little salt and freshly ground black pepper to taste.

Transfer the baked sweet potatoes to a large plate and serve with the spicy guacamole.

ASIAN STIR FRY

Asian stir fries are among the quickest meals to make – perfect for when you have little time to cook but still want something tasty and nutritious. Vegetables are the main act here, and I like to use bok choi, a typical Chinese vegetable, which is one of the first leafy greens that comes into season in the spring.

Serves 3 or 4

☆	☆	☆	☆	☆	☆	☆
12 oz. rice noodles	4 heads of bok choy, white stems separated from the greens	2 garlic cloves, chopped	½ red chile, sliced or chopped (deseeded for a milder version)	1 thumb-sized piece of fresh ginger, peeled and finely chopped	4 tablespoons tamari or soy sauce	Sweet and Salty Cashews (page 152), chopped

Cook the noodles in boiling water following the package instructions. When done, drain, rinse with cold water and let sit.

Chop the white stems of the bok choy and cook them in a wok over a high heat with a splash of water, stirring constantly. After 3 to 4 minutes, add the garlic, chile, and ginger and keep stirring. After a minute, add the noodles, bok choy greens, and a splash of water if needed. Mixed well until the noodles are warm (about 2 minutes), then add the soy sauce or tamari. Toss well.

Serve scattered with the chopped cashews. You can also drizzle with some toasted sesame oil, if you like.

OIL-FREE PISTOU WITH PASTA

Almost everyone is familiar with pesto – the North Italian basil sauce – but less well known is the French version, pistou. It has the same base as pesto, but it lacks the Parmesan and pine nuts of its Italian counterpart. This version uses avocado rather than oil to create a rich, creamy texture. Pistou is normally quite heavy on the garlic, which gives a potent taste, although you can use less if you prefer. Broccoli and green beans work great here, but you could also use asparagus or seasonal beans.

Serves 4

☆	☆	☆	☆	☆	☆	☆
14 oz. short pasta	14 oz. green beans, cut in half or into thirds	1 head of broccoli, cut into small florets	2 large bunches of basil (each 3 oz.), roughly chopped	¼ avocado	4 to 6 garlic cloves, chopped	Juice of 1 lemon

Cook the pasta according to the package instructions in plenty of boiling water. Bring another pot of water to a boil and add the green beans. Cook for 7 to 8 minutes with the lid on, and after 3 to 4 minutes, add the broccoli, then drain and let sit.

Meanwhile, make the pistou. Put the basil, avocado, garlic, lemon juice, and 1 teaspoon salt in a blender and add about ¼ cup of water. Process until smooth. Add more water a tablespoon at a time if it needs loosening.

Drain the pasta, reserving 3 tablespoons of the cooking water. Add the vegetables, pistou, and reserved cooking water (it will make your pasta creamier) to the pasta and mix so the pasta is evenly coated. Serve immediately.

★ Optional extras
You can also add some Pine Nut Parmesan (page 42) to this dish.

★ Tip
You can use red lentil, chickpea, rice, or traditional orecchiette for the pasta. Leftover pistou is great on a sandwich with some fresh tomato and avocado slices.

INDIAN SWEET POTATO ROSTI WITH ONION SALAD

A lot of traditional Indian food is vegan and I'm quite fond of a fusion twist, so here I've combined curried sweet potatoes with the Swiss dish called rosti.

Makes 8 to 10

☆	☆	☆	☆	☆	☆	☆
1 lb. sweet potato, peeled and grated	3 red onions, thinly sliced	1 tablespoon garam masala	¼ teaspoon chili powder	3 tablespoons plus 1 teaspoon chopped fresh cilantro	3 tablespoons chickpea flour	Juice of ½ lemon or 1 lime

Preheat the oven to 300°F.

Rinse the grated sweet potato in a strainer and drain. In a large bowl, mix the potato with a third of the thinly sliced red onion. Add ½ teaspoon of salt, the garam masala, chili powder, 3 tablespoons of chopped cilantro and the chickpea flour and stir well to combine.

Place a nonstick skillet over medium–high heat and add some coconut oil. Form a rosti by taking about 5 tablespoons of the sweet potato mixture and shaping it into a small burger. Lay the rosti in the pan and press down well with the back of a spatula to flatten. Let it cook for about 4 to 5 minutes, then carefully flip it over and cook the other side for an additional 3 to 4 minutes. Repeat until all the mixture is used. Keep the cooked rostis warm in the oven on a plate covered with foil.

Make a small onion salad by mixing the remaining sliced onion with the lemon or lime juice, ¼ teaspoon of salt, and a teaspoon of chopped fresh cilantro.

Serve the rosti with the salad and some Homemade Yogurt (page 151).

PORTOBELLO SATAY WITH PEANUT SAUCE

Dutch cuisine is greatly influenced by the food of its former colonies, such as the Indonesian-style peanut satay sauce. Although traditionally served with Satay – small portions of goat or chicken on skewers – the peanut sauce has become such a regular feature of Dutch cuisine that it is eaten with almost everything. It's probably the second most popular sauce in Holland after mayonnaise. This satay is made with Portobello mushrooms – ideal for cooking either in a grill pan or on the barbecue. Served with some toasted shredded coconut for some crunch and a side of fried rice, it makes a really delicious meal!

Serves 4

☆	☆	☆	☆	☆	☆	☆
6 portobello mushrooms, cleaned and stems removed	¾ cup peanut butter	½–1 teaspoon chili powder (to taste)	1 thumb-sized piece of ginger, peeled and grated	Juice of 1 lime	2 tablespoons nama shoyu or tamari	3½ cups shredded or flaked coconut

If you are using wooden skewers, soak them in hot water for 10 to 15 minutes.

Slice the mushrooms into long thick strips and thread each slice (lengthwise) onto a skewer. Sprinkle over a little salt and let sit while you make the peanut sauce.

In a blender, mix together the peanut butter, chili powder, grated ginger, lime juice, nama shoyu or tamari, and 1⅔ cups hot water until smooth.

Heat a grill pan and cook the mushroom skewers for about 6 to 7 minutes on each side.

Meanwhile, toast the coconut. Heat a nonstick or heavy-bottomed pan over medium heat, add the dried coconut, and stir frequently until it begins to turn golden brown. Remove from the heat.

Serve the mushroom satay with the peanut butter and toasted coconut on top.

★ Variation
Add 1 tablespoon maple syrup for a sweeter version of this peanut sauce.

TASTE OF THE SEA PATTIES

These patties have a wonderful taste of the sea due to the seaweed, and are better for your health and for the ocean than fish. Seaweed has become hugely popular recently and I love its umami taste. It's also packed with nutrients: high in vitamin K, calcium, and iron. A sheet of nori reportedly contains the same amount of omega-3 fatty acids as two avocados, plus there's an almost unlimited resource of it in our oceans.

Makes 8 small patties

☆	☆	☆	☆	☆	☆
5 oz. cooked (3 oz. dry) quinoa	¾ cup cooked (½ x 14 oz. can) white beans (e.g. cannellini)	1 tablespoon Aonori (crumbled nori) or dulse powder	1 tablespoon mustard	Zest of ½ lemon	3 tablespoons chopped chives

Put all the ingredients in a food-processor and add salt and freshly ground black pepper to taste. Process until well blended, then divide the mixture into eight equal portions and form into patties. If you have time, place the patties in the freezer for 10 to 15 minutes to firm up.

Heat a nonstick ceramic skillet over medium heat and brush with a little coconut oil.

Place the patties in the pan and cook for 3 minutes on each side (you may have to do this in batches). They are ready when they have formed a golden crust.

The patties can be served with your favorite condiment, such as ketchup, Lemon Tahini Dressing (page 160), or Spicy Cucumber Pickles (page 164).

GREEN QUINOA BOWLS

Quinoa is a tiny grain that has a slight nutty flavor and is gluten-free. You can get all kinds of varieties, including white, black, and red. Originating from South America, it's become very popular in recent years, particularly among vegetarians and vegans. Combined with greens and beans, quinoa makes a fast and fresh meal.

Serves 4

☆	☆	☆	☆	☆	☆
7 oz. quinoa	1 lb. curly kale or cavolo nero	3 lemons	6 oz. peas, fresh or frozen	2 avocados	1 bunch of tarragon or parsley, chopped

Rinse the quinoa and cook according to the package instructions in salted water.

Meanwhile, tear the kale or cavalo nero leaves into small pieces and place in a large bowl with a pinch of salt and the juice of half a lemon. Massage the leaves with your hands for 2 to 3 minutes to soften.

Blanch the peas in boiling water for about 1 minute, then drain.

Slice the two remaining lemons in half and cook them, cut side down, in a hot grill pan or nonstick skillet for 5 to 6 minutes. This will caramelize the skin and soften the flesh.

Peel and remove the pits from the avocados and slice the flesh.

When the quinoa is done, divide it between four bowls. Top with the kale, peas, avocado, and tarragon or parsley. Add salt and freshly ground black pepper to taste and drizzle over some olive oil. Serve with the grilled lemons.

LENTIL & POMEGRANATE SALAD

Lentils have to be my favorite quick-cooking beans: they don't require soaking, can be ready in about 20 minutes, and make a great base for a substantial meal. This delicious dish uses the flavors of the Middle East and brings some sunshine in winter, when pomegranate season is at its peak.

Serves 4

☆	☆	☆	☆	☆	☆	☆
1¼ cups Puy or other firm lentils (e.g. beluga), rinsed	1 large bunch of parsley, chopped	1 large bunch of fresh mint, chopped	Seeds of 1 pomegranate (see Tip)	1 tablespoon chopped preserved lemon peel, plus 1 tablespoon juice	1 garlic clove, chopped	1 batch Almond Feta (page 149)

Cook the lentils in 3 cups of water according to the package instructions. Be careful not to overcook: the lentils should be tender but not broken and mushy.

Drain the lentils and place in a large bowl. Add the parsley, mint, pomegranate seeds, chopped preserved lemon peel and juice, garlic, and 3 tablespoons of olive oil. Season with a little salt and freshly ground black pepper (the almond feta is very salty, so go easy on the salt).

Mix until combined. Scatter over the almond feta and serve warm.

★ Tips
To remove the seeds from a pomegranate, cut it into quarters and, with your fingers, remove the red seeds from both the skin and the membrane over a bowl filled with water. When you drop the seeds into the water, the tiny bits of skin that are still stuck to the seeds will float to the top and the seeds will sink to the bottom. Skim the bits from the surface and strain the water from the clean seeds.

★ Variation
Substitute the almond feta with ¾ cups raw pistachios, peeled and chopped.

FENNEL & SAFFRON STEW

This fennel and saffron dish can be ready and on your table within 30 minutes, and will have you dreaming of the South of France on a sunny day. Serve it on its own or with steamed potatoes, bread, or cooked grains.

Serves 3 to 4

☆	☆	☆	☆	☆	☆	☆
1 pinch of saffron threads	1 lb. fennel, including green fronds	2 garlic cloves, finely chopped	Leaves of 2 sprigs of thyme	1 bay leaf	4 tomatoes, peeled and chopped, or 14 oz. can of chopped tomatoes	1¼ cups cooked chickpeas (14 oz. can, drained)

Place the saffron threads in a cup, pour over ¼ cup of freshly boiled water and leave to soak.

Cut the fennel into quarters and remove most of the inner core, leaving just enough for the fennel to stay intact. Slice the quarters vertically into strips. Chop the green fennel fronds and let sit.

Place a pot over a medium heat and add the garlic, fennel, thyme, bay leaf, and a couple of tablespoons of water. Gently cook for about 3 minutes. Add the chopped tomatoes and 1¾ cups water and bring to a boil. Reduce the heat and simmer for 20 minutes.

Add the chickpeas and cook for an additional 5 minutes. Serve garnished with the additional fennel fronds.

★ Variation
Add 1 tablespoon capers. If using the salted variety, leave to soak in some water for 10 minutes before using. These can be added with the tomatoes.

SURINAME-STYLE CURRY

Amsterdam has a greater diversity of restaurants than any other European city, and I'm always inspired by the cuisines on offer: French, Italian, Greek, Chinese, Indonesian, Afghan, and more. Many of these restaurants were started by people from former Dutch colonies, of which Suriname was one. This Suriname-style curry is traditionally served with a chickpea flatbread called roti, but is also great with cooked brown rice or quinoa.

Serves 4 to 6

☆	☆	☆	☆	☆	☆	☆
1 medium onion, chopped	1 tablespoon chopped fresh red chile (optional)	2 tablespoons curry powder, any variety	1 lb. 5 oz. small potatoes, peeled and cut in half	3 cups green beans, tips removed, cut into ¾-inch pieces	1 block of tofu (9 oz.), cut into ½-inch cubes	1 cup coconut milk

Cook the onion and chile in a pan with a couple of tablespoons of water until the onions are translucent. If needed, add a splash more water from time to time to prevent burning.

Add the curry powder and stir, then add the potatoes and mix well until coated.

Add 2 cups water and ½ teaspoon of salt. Bring to a boil with the lid on and leave to simmer for 10 minutes on medium heat.

Add the green beans and cook for another 5 to 6 minutes.

All should be cooked now; if not, give it another 2 to 3 minutes. Add the tofu and coconut milk and leave to simmer on low for 2 minutes. Taste for seasoning then serve.

★ Optional extras
The Spicy Cucumber Pickles on page 164 work great with this dish.
To give it more kick, add some sambal oelek or Asian Sweet and Spicy sauce (see page 163).

NOODLES WITH CARROT MISO SAUCE

During my university years in Amsterdam my favorite restaurant was Shizen, which served wonderful vegan food. Years later I discovered that Amy Chaplin, one of my favorite bloggers and authors, had worked there in the same period. Her book, *At Home in the Whole Food Kitchen*, contains lots of inspirational recipes, and this is my take on her tasty and versatile carrot sauce.

Serves 4

☆	☆	☆	☆	☆	☆	☆
9 oz. carrots, peeled and grated	½ cup light miso paste	¼ cup tahini	1 tablespoon yuzu vinegar or rice vinegar	1 thumb-sized piece of ginger, peeled and grated	12 oz. noodles (see Variations)	1¼ cups cooked edamame beans

First make the sauce. Blend the grated carrots, miso, tahini, vinegar, ginger, and 1 cup of water in a high-speed blender until smooth. Taste, add more salt if needed, then let sit.

Cook the noodles in boiling water according to the package instructions. When ready, drain and rinse.

Divide the sauce between four bowls, then top with the noodles and beans and serve immediately.

★ Tips

Any noodles will work, but black rice noodles or zucchini noodles are great options. If you can't find edamame beans, substitute smoked tofu or stir-fried tempeh.

The yuzu vinegar can be replaced by equal parts of clementine juice and lime juice. Add some more vegetables to this dish, such as pickles, cucumber, nori flakes, sesame seeds and sprouts, or micro herbs.

☆
START

☆
FRESH

☆
FAST

★
NOURISH

☆
GATHER

☆
SWEET

☆
BASIC

SPICY CARROT & CHICKPEA STEW

The easiest recipes are ones that can be put in a single pan and left on the heat to simmer, providing some quiet time to enjoy a moment of relaxation. This dish is based on North African flavors: harissa, chickpeas, and olives. Harissa is a fragrant and hot chili sauce that includes spices such as cumin, coriander, and caraway, and it is commonly used in North African and Middle Eastern kitchens to flavor stews, soups, and couscous dishes. Simple and flavorsome, this stew will take you to exotic places with every mouthful.

Serves 4

☆	☆	☆	☆	☆	☆	☆
1 medium onion, chopped	1½ to 2 tablespoons harissa paste	14 oz. can chopped tomatoes	6 medium carrots, cut into ½-inch slices	¾ oz. fresh cilantro, leaves and stems chopped separately	2½ cups cooked chickpeas (2 x 14 oz. cans, drained and rinsed)	3 oz. pitted olives, whole

Cook the onions in a pan over medium heat with a splash of water until they are soft, but not brown, about 5 to 10 minutes. Add the harissa paste, ½ a teaspoon salt and a good grinding of black pepper. Mix well, then add the tomatoes, carrots, chopped cilantro stems, and 1 cup water. Bring to a boil, then reduce the heat to low and simmer for 10 minutes until the carrots are tender.

Add the chickpeas and olives and cook for an additional 5 minutes. Taste for seasoning and add more salt or pepper if needed. If you like it hot, add another ½ teaspoon (or more) of harissa paste. Stir again and serve scattered with the cilantro leaves.

★ Serving suggestion
Serve with couscous, bulgur wheat, quinoa, and a dollop of Homemade Yogurt (page 151) to cool down this spicy dish.

BUCKWHEAT RISOTTO WITH ASPARAGUS

This nourishing risotto has all the flavors of spring with fresh asparagus, but also a warmth and creaminess that is perfect on gray rainy days. Buckwheat is a gluten-free grain that is actually a member of the rhubarb family! Unlike a traditional rice risotto, it doesn't need that much stirring to become creamy and lush – minimum effort, maximum result.

Serves 4

☆	☆	☆	☆	☆	☆
1 medium onion, finely chopped	2 stalks of celery, finely chopped	2⅓ cups buckwheat, washed and drained	6 cups water or Vegetable Stock (page 155)	1 lb. asparagus, hard ends of spears discarded	4 tablespoons chopped herbs, e.g. dill, tarragon or basil

Cook the onion and celery in a pot over medium heat with a splash of water for 5 to 10 minutes until soft and glazed, adding more water if needed.

Add the buckwheat and water or vegetable stock and bring to a boil. Reduce the heat to medium and leave to simmer for 20 to 25 minutes, stirring once in a while.

Cut each asparagus spear in thirds, then blanch for 2 minutes in a small pan of boiling water. Drain.

When the buckwheat is soft and creamy, add the asparagus (reserving a few pieces to garnish) and fresh herbs and stir thoroughly. Serve immediately.

★ Variation
For ultimate creaminess, stir ½ cup Savory Cashew Cream (page 150) mixed with 5 tablespoons nutritional yeast into the risotto with the asparagus and chopped herbs.

MUSHROOM POLENTA TART

Chilly autumn days always make me crave creamy, earthy, and comforting food. Mushrooms are perfect, and if I'm lucky, a French neighbor will give me a bag of freshly foraged "trompettes de la mort" or "pieds de mouton."

Serves 4

☆	☆	☆	☆	☆	☆	☆
¾ cup polenta	¾ cup chestnut flour	4 cups water or Vegetable Stock (page 155)	8 cups (26 oz.) mixed mushrooms, cleaned	3 garlic cloves, finely chopped	1 bunch of parsley, chopped	Zest and juice of ½ lemon

Preheat the oven to 350°F and line a baking tray with parchment paper.

Mix together the polenta and chestnut flour and cook in salted water or stock, according to the polenta package instructions. Stir often to prevent burning.

Once cooked, gently and evenly spread it out on the lined baking sheet in a layer about ½-inch thick. Bake for 35 to 45 minutes until crisp.

Roughly chop the mushrooms and cook for 8 to 10 minutes in a pot on a high heat with two-thirds of the chopped garlic, 2 tablespoons chopped parsley, the lemon juice and a pinch of salt. The salt will release the moisture of the mushrooms, so be careful with adding extra water. If needed, add 1 tablespoon at a time. If the mushrooms are very wet, drain off excess liquid so the polenta base doesn't become soggy. Let sit.

When the crust is ready, spread the mushrooms on top and bake in the oven for an additional 5 minutes.

Meanwhile, make the gremolata by mixing the remaining chopped parsley and garlic with the lemon zest.

Remove the tart from the oven, sprinkle the gremolata on top and serve.

★ Tip
You can prepare the crust in advance, then chill before use and bake it while making the mushroom ragout. If chestnut flour isn't available, double the quantity of polenta.

RED CABBAGE "STEAKS" WITH DUKKAH

My husband eats almost everything, except red cabbage. Pairing it with apples is a classic Dutch combination, but even this can't persuade him! Determined to change his mind, these "steaks" finally made him appreciate how delicious they can be – and he loves them!

Serves 4 to 6

☆	☆	☆	☆	☆	☆	☆
1 small red cabbage, cut through the core into ½- to 1-inch thick "steaks"	6 tablespoons orange juice	1 cup walnuts (or use almonds or pistachios)	⅓ cup sesame seeds	3 tablespoons coriander seeds	3 tablespoons cumin seeds	Homemade Yogurt (page 151), to serve (optional)

Preheat the oven to 400°F.

Line a baking sheet with parchment paper and lay the cabbage on it. Sprinkle with orange juice, salt and pepper. Try not to overlap the "steaks" as this will prevent them from cooking evenly. Cover with foil and bake for 20 minutes, then remove the foil and cook for an additional 10 minutes until tender.

While the cabbage is roasting, make the dukkah. Toast the nuts and seeds in a dry pan over low heat for about 7 to 8 minutes, stirring occasionally until fragrant. Grind with ¾ teaspoon salt in a mortar and pestle or food-processor. Be careful not to over-process: the dukkah should be crumbly and not smooth like a nut butter.

Serve the steaks with 2 teaspoons of dukkah scattered over the top and, if you wish, a dollop of homemade yogurt.

★ Tip
When cutting the cabbage, make sure that you cut through the core, leaving it in place, so that the "steaks" hold together.

★ Optional extra
These "steaks" are great with the Creamy Winter Mash on page 85.

MEXICAN BLACK BEAN CHILI

The first time I went to a Mexican restaurant I immediately loved the flavor combinations; they're so fresh and punchy. To get the real essence of Mexican food you need a base of cumin, smoked chili, and oregano.

Serves 4

☆	☆	☆	☆	☆	☆	☆
2 large onions, chopped	3 peppers (any color), cut into ½-inch chunks	3 teaspoons oregano	2½ teaspoons ground cumin	2 to 3 teaspoons hot smoked chili such as chipotle (or smoked paprika)	14 oz. tomatoes, peeled and chopped, or 1 x 14 oz. can chopped tomatoes	4 cups cooked black beans, drained, (or 3 x 14 oz. can)

Cook the onions in a pot over medium heat with a splash of water for 5 to 8 minutes until they are brown and caramelized.

Add the paprika, cumin, and oregano and stir for a minute or so, then stir in the tomatoes and cook for 2 to 3 minutes.

Add the black beans, bring to a boil with the lid on, then reduce the heat to low and leave to simmer for 20 to 25 minutes. If you want, roughly blend the chili to get a smoother consistency.

Season to taste and serve immediately.

★ Optional extras
You can serve the chili with fresh lime, chopped fresh cilantro, Spicy Guacamole (page 58), or Savory Cashew Cream (page 150), accompanied with tortillas or in an oven-baked (sweet) potato.

CREAMY WINTER MASH

Mashed potato is arguably the ultimate comfort food. In the Netherlands it's often served mixed with raw greens and called "stamppot," which translates to "pressed or mashed dish." Although traditionally loaded with butter and milk, the potatoes and greens are the real stars of the show so it makes a great vegan dish. This version uses vegetables that are often ignored by the Dutch.

Serves 4

☆	☆	☆	☆	☆
4½ lbs. mixed winter vegetables (e.g. celery root, parsnip, cauliflower)	1 bay leaf (optional)	4 cups water or Vegetable Stock (page 155)	4 tablespoons nutritional yeast	¼ cup Savory Cashew Cream (page 150, optional)

Peel the vegetables and roughly chop them into same-sized pieces, then place them and the bay leaf in a large pot with the water or stock, bring to a boil and leave to simmer until tender. Depending on the size of the vegetables, this will take 10 to 15 minutes.

Drain the vegetables, reserving about 1½ cups of the cooking liquid. Mash the vegetables using a potato masher or in a food-processor, adding some of the cooking liquid to make it smooth. Add in the nutritional yeast and season with salt and freshly ground black pepper to taste. If you wish, you can add the cashew cream for extra richness.

★ Variation
If you like, you can stir in 1 lb. 10 oz. chopped greens, such as kale, purslane, turnip tops, arugula, or spinach.

★ Optional extras
This mash can be served with cooked beans or sautéed mushrooms. You can also combine it with the Red Cabbage Steak on page 82 or the Smokin' Burgers on page 112.

LENTIL & PORCINI RAGOUT

Dried porcini mushrooms give this ragout a deep, satisfying taste and are a perfect match with the earthy cavolo nero. It's best to use Black beluga or French Puy lentils as they will keep their shape when cooked. Serve on top of a roasted sweet potato, or with your choice of pasta or cooked grain.

Serves 4

☆	☆	☆	☆	☆	☆	☆
4 medium sweet potatoes	¼ cup dried porcini mushrooms	1¼ cup beluga or Puy lentils	3 garlic cloves, finely chopped	2 tablespoons herbes de Provence	14 oz. can chopped tomatoes	1 lb. cavalo nero, torn or cut into smaller pieces

Preheat the oven to 400°F. Place the sweet potatoes on a baking sheet and cook for 45 minutes until tender.

Place the dried mushrooms in a heat-resistant bowl and pour over 4 cups boiling water, leaving to rehydrate for 15 to 20 minutes. Drain and reserve the soaking liquid, then roughly chop the mushrooms.

Wash the lentils in a fine mesh strainer then place them in a pot with 4 cups of water. Bring to a boil with the lid on, then reduce the heat and leave to simmer for 20 to 25 minutes. Drain any remaining cooking liquid and let sit.

In a pot over a medium heat, cook the mushrooms with their soaking liquid and the garlic. After a minute, add the herbes de Provence and the tomatoes and cook for another 2 to 3 minutes. Add the lentils and season with salt and freshly ground black pepper. Bring to a boil, then reduce the heat to low and simmer for 15 minutes. If it looks too dry, add some more water. When the lentils are cooked, add the cavolo nero or Savoy cabbage. Cook for an additional 8 to 10 minutes, until soft and done.

Remove the sweet potatoes from the oven, make a deep slit in the top of each one and open them up a bit. Fill with the ragout and serve immediately.

★ Tips
I always use a strainer lined with a clean dish towel or cheesecloth to catch the dirt or sand from the mushrooms when draining them after soaking.

★ Serving suggestion
I like to serve this ragout inside roasted sweet potatoes, but you can serve it with your favorite pasta or any other cooked grains as well.

ROASTED CHERRY TOMATO QUICHE

Savory quiches are a staple of French feasts, picnics, and bakeries. Traditionally, the key ingredients are flour, milk, and egg, and the well-known quiche Lorraine also includes bacon and cheese. Although fillings can vary widely, I've never seen a vegan one. This cherry tomato version is the perfect alternative.

Serves 4

☆	☆	☆	☆	☆	☆	☆
1 head of garlic	2½ cups oat flakes	½ cup ground almonds	3 tablespoons ground chia seeds or linseeds	1 lb. 10 oz. cherry tomatoes	2 tablespoons balsamic vinegar	1¼ cup cooked lima beans or 1 x 14 oz. can, drained

Preheat the oven 350°F.

Slice off the very top of the garlic bulb so a few of the cloves are exposed. Wrap in foil and fold up the edges to make a little pouch. Sprinkle some salt and freshly ground black pepper and drizzle a little water on top. Close the foil to seal in the garlic bulb, then place on a baking sheet and cook in the oven for 50 to 60 minutes until soft.

Meanwhile, make the quiche case. Grind the oats in a food-processor until you have oatmeal flour. Combine with the almonds, chia, ¼ teaspoon salt, and ⅔ cup boiled water in a bowl and mix well to form a dough. Do this quickly or the chia seeds will soak up all the water and the dough will become stiff. It may be a little sticky, but that's fine. Press the dough into a tart pan with a removable bottom. Start by covering the bottom then continue up the sides, making sure the dough is evenly distributed.

Toss the cherry tomatoes in the vinegar with some salt and pepper and spread out on a baking sheet. Roast the tomatoes and bake the quiche crust in the oven for 20 to 25 minutes. (Remove the cherry tomatoes when they burst and start to caramelize).

When the garlic is cooked, squeeze the flesh from each clove and mix together with the beans in a food-processor or blender until very smooth. Season to taste. Spread this mixture evenly over the bottom of the quiche case. Lay the roasted tomatoes on top then return the quiche to the oven and cook for an additional 20 minutes.

Remove the quiche from the oven and let it cool a little before serving.

★ Variations
Replace the tomatoes with roasted winter vegetables like pumpkin, carrots, or beets, or try using roasted asparagus in spring. You could also use the Almond Curd (page 147) from the basic chapter instead of the bean filling.

PARSNIP & LEEK SOUP

Vegetable soup is very different in the Netherlands and France – while the Dutch favor broth with whole vegetables, French soup is generally a much thicker and blended smooth. This French-style soup uses typically autumn and winter flavors, with fresh herbs giving a wonderful aroma.

Serves 4 to 6

☆	☆	☆	☆	☆	☆	☆
1 leek, sliced	1 bay leaf	1 tablespoon finely chopped cilantro	1 tablespoon fresh thyme leaves	4 parsnips, peeled and chopped into chunks	4 cups water or Vegetable Stock (page 155)	Herb and Lemon Chickpea Croutons (page 156)

Cook the leek in a large pan over medium heat with the herbs and a splash of water for 6 to 8 minutes, until soft. Add the parsnip, stir and cook for an additional 2 minutes, then add the water or stock and bring to a boil. Turn down the heat and leave to simmer for 15 to 20 minutes with the lid on until the parsnip is tender.

Discard the bay leaf and blend the soup until smooth. Place the soup back on low heat for a couple of minutes to heat through.

Season to taste with salt and freshly ground black pepper.

Ladle the soup into bowls, add the croutons, and serve immediately.

★ Variations
Replace the chickpea croutons with cooked chestnuts: their flavor is perfect with this soup. If you wish, you can even add a swirl of Savory Cashew Cream (page 150) before serving too.

SWEET POTATO GNOCCHI WITH ARUGULA "PESTO"

Italian gnocchi is a delicious way of eating sweet potato, and it goes particularly well with arugula pesto. The strong, peppery, and slightly bitter taste goes perfectly with the sweetness of the potato. You can use orange, purple, or white sweet potatoes, depending on what is available.

Serves 3 to 4

☆	☆	☆	☆	☆	☆	☆
1 lb. sweet potatoes (about 2 medium)	¾ cup buckwheat flour (or use spelt flour)	3½ oz. arugula, roughly chopped	¾ cup sunflower seeds	Juice of ½ lemon	2 garlic cloves	3 tablespoons nutritional yeast

Preheat the oven to 400°F. Prick the sweet potatoes with a fork and bake them in the oven for about 45 to 60 minutes until tender.

Slice open the sweet potatoes as soon as they are cool enough to handle, scoop out the flesh into a bowl, and mash with a fork or a potato ricer. Add the flour and ½ teaspoon salt and combine thoroughly with a fork.

With clean hands, form the dough into a smooth ball. Try not to overwork it as this will result in tough and hard gnocchi. Divide the ball into 2 portions, roll each into a sausage shape, and cut into 1 1/4" pieces. Press down lightly on each gnocchi with the back of a fork as this will help the sauce cling to your gnocchi. You can use these gnocchi right away, store them in the refrigerator for up to 2 days, or freeze them.

Next make the pesto. Place the arugula, sunflower seeds, lemon juice, garlic, nutritional yeast, and salt and pepper in a food-processor. Turn it on and gradually add ⅓ cup hot water. You may need to scrape down the edges from time to time and add a splash more water. Process until you have a pesto-like consistency. Add salt to taste.

Bring a large pot of water to a boil. Add the gnocchi and cook for about 2 minutes, or a little longer if cooking from frozen. The gnocchi are ready when they float to the top of the boiling water. Drain.

Stir the pesto with the gnocchi until thoroughly coated and serve immediately.

ROOT VEGETABLE BOULANGÈRE

Boulangère is a classic French oven-baked potato dish. The name dates from when it would have been made at the local bakery (*boulanger*) because of a lack of home ovens. This version uses a mixture of winter root vegetables rather than just the traditional potato, and although it takes a while to cook the taste is worth the wait!

Serves 4

☆	☆	☆
3 lbs. 5 oz. mixed winter root vegetables (e.g. parsnip, potato, carrot)	1¾ Vegetable Stock (page 155)	3 tablespoons mixed chopped sage, rosemary, and thyme

Preheat the oven to 400°F.

Peel and roughly chop your chosen vegetables and lay them in an ovenproof dish (about 8 x 12 x 2 inches deep). Pour the stock over the vegetables and scatter the herbs on top.

Cook on the highest shelf of the oven for about 1 hour, or until the top turns golden and crisp and the vegetables are tender. If the top starts to turn too dark, cover with foil. Take out of the oven and serve.

★ Tip
Onions also make a tasty addition to the mix of winter vegetables.

ROASTED PUMPKIN, ROMANESCO & LIMA BEANS

This dish is based on a meal I ate in Amsterdam at a small shop called Olive and Cookie. The couple that runs it serve delicious fresh food, with lots of attention, love, and detail. This is my take of one of their fantastic dishes.

Serves 4

☆	☆	☆	☆	☆	☆	☆
1 pumpkin (approx. 2 lbs.), peeled, deseeded and cut into ¾-inch thick slices	1 head of romanesco (or cauliflower), washed and cut into florets	3 teaspoons white balsamic vinegar or orange juice	1½ teaspoons ground cumin	1½ teaspoons smoked sweet paprika	1¼ cup cooked lima beans, or 1 x 14 oz. can, drained	14 oz. arugula or watercress

Preheat the oven to 350°F. Line a baking sheet with parchment paper.

Put the pumpkin and romanesco in a bowl and add the balsamic vinegar, cumin, and smoked paprika and season with salt and freshly ground black pepper. Stir to evenly coat, then spread the vegetables out on the baking sheet and place in the oven for 25 minutes.

Remove the baking sheet from the oven, stir the vegetables, and add the lima beans. Return to the oven and cook for an additional 10 to 15 minutes, until the pumpkin and cauliflower are tender.

Scatter the arugula or watercress on top and serve.

★ Optional extras
This dish is delicious with some cooked grains and the Mustard Maple Sauce (page 160) or Lemon Tahini Dressing (page 160).

PEARL BARLEY & CLEMENTINE BRUSSELS SPROUT SALAD

Salads don't just have to be for the summer. As the weather gets colder, simply add grains, beans, and warm seasonal vegetables to make a nourishing and comforting winter meal. This dish uses Chioggia "candy cane" beet, named because of the distinctive pattern on the inside of the vegetable.

Serves 4

☆	☆	☆	☆	☆	☆	☆
5 oz. pearl barley	2 lbs. 4 oz. Brussels sprouts	Juice of 2 clementines	1 teaspoon fennel seeds	1 Chioggia beet, finely sliced	½ cup pumpkin seeds	3 tablespoons olive oil (optional)

Cook the pearl barley in water or stock according to the package instructions. Drain (if necessary) and let sit.

Remove and discard the outer leaves of the Brussels sprouts and thinly slice them on a mandoline. Quickly stir-fry the sliced Brussels sprouts with 3 tablespoons of clementine juice, the fennel seeds, and salt and freshly ground black pepper to taste. This will take only a minute or two—there should still be some crunch to the Brussels sprouts.

Transfer the sprouts to a bowl and add the pearl barley and Chioggia beets.

Dry-roast the pumpkin seeds in a hot pan, stirring often to prevent them burning, until they pop and are golden brown. Add the pumpkin seeds to the bowl and drizzle the remaining clementine juice and olive oil on top, if using. Add salt and pepper to taste, then gently toss to combine and serve.

★ Tip
It's easiest to slice the beets using a mandoline

☆ START ☆ FRESH ☆ FAST ☆ NOURISH ★ **GATHER** ☆ SWEET ☆ BASIC

PILAF-STUFFED TOMATOES

These tomatoes are perfect for a shared summer meal with friends. You can prepare them in advance and cook just before serving, meaning you are free to join your guests and not be stuck in the kitchen. Serve with a salad for a tasty but simple meal.

Serves 4

☆	☆	☆	☆	☆	☆	☆
⅓ cup pine nuts	1 medium onion, finely chopped	½ teaspoon allspice	⅓ cup currants, soaked	¼ cup fresh dill, chopped	10½ oz. wholegrain basmati rice	8 medium-sized tomatoes

Soak the basmati rice for at least 30 minutes, then rinse and drain.

Preheat the oven to 350°F.

Heat a skillet over medium heat, add the pine nuts and toast until golden brown. Let sit.

To make the pilaf, cook the chopped onion with a splash of water in a medium-sized pot over medium heat until soft, adding a little more water if needed. Add the allspice, currants, toasted pine nuts, half the dill and salt, and gently mix. Add the basmati rice, stir well, then add 3 cups water. Bring to a boil, then reduce the heat and cook the rice for the time indicated on the package.

Meanwhile, cut the tops off the tomatoes and scoop out the seeds and core. Once the pilaf is cooked, fill the tomatoes with this rice mixture. Place the tomatoes on a baking sheet and cook in the oven for 15 to 20 minutes.

Scatter the remaining dill over the tomatoes to serve.

★ Optional extras
Eat the tomatoes with a good squeeze of lemon juice or a dollop of yogurt, chili, or tahini sauce.

FILLED FRENCH BREAD

This derives from the traditional Provençal *pain bagnat*: hollowed-out bread filled with typical Mediterranean ingredients such as tomatoes, tuna, and onions, and weighted down so that the bread soaks up all the flavors. Homemade Pistou (page 62), grilled peppers, and fresh juicy tomatoes make this version very special. It's also perfect to make in advance for a picnic.

Serves 4

☆	☆	☆	☆	☆	☆	☆
3 red peppers (or 1 jar of roasted red peppers)	1 whole, round rustic sourdough bread	1 batch Pistou (page 62) or store-bought pesto	1 batch Almond Ricotta (page 146)	4 ripe tomatoes, sliced	1 red onion, sliced into rings	5 oz. black olives, pitted

Start by roasting the red peppers. If you have a gas stovetop, char them directly over the flame to give them a delicious smoky flavor. Insert a fork into the green top of a pepper and turn the burner to high. Hold the pepper above the flame, turning it until the skin on all sides has turned black. Alternatively, you can roast them on the barbecue or under the broiler of your oven. When the pepper is soft, put it in a heatproof bowl and cover with plastic wrap to let the steam loosen the skin. Repeat the process until all peppers are cooked. When cool enough to handle, remove the skin. You may need to do this under running water.

Cut the top from the bread and scoop it out until you are left with a hollow loaf with a crust about ½-inch thick. Save the remaining bread for making, for example, croutons for another recipe.

Now start filling your bread. First spread a layer of pistou on the bottom. Then add a couple of pieces of grilled pepper, some almond ricotta or feta, two or three slices of tomato, some onion rings, and some olives. Repeat all the steps until your bread is filled up. Replace the bread "lid" and wrap the loaf in plastic wrap. Place it onto a cutting board, put another cutting board or large plate on top of it and weight it down, for example with a heavy cookbook. Leave for 1 hour.

Unwrap the bread and serve cut into thick slices.

★ Variation
Substitute the Almond Ricotta for a piece of crumbled Almond Feta (page 149).

EGGPLANT ESCABECHE

Escabeche is a well-known dish in both the Mediterranean and Latin American. It normally refers to fish that has been marinated in an acidic sauce overnight, then served cold. For this vegan version, eggplants are the perfect substitute: they are sturdy and absorb flavors very well. It's tastiest at the end of summer or the beginning of autumn when eggplants are at their best.

Serves 4

☆	☆	☆	☆	☆	☆	☆
2 medium eggplants	1 bunch of parsley	1 red onion, sliced	A few sprigs of fresh thyme	½ cup red wine vinegar or apple cider vinegar	1 teaspoon coriander seeds	1 teaspoon whole peppercorns

Cut the eggplants lengthways into eight large pieces. Place in a steamer and steam in a pan for about 10 minutes, until soft.

Meanwhile, prepare the vinegar sauce. Chop the parsley stalks and reserve the leaves. Put the parsley stalks, onion, thyme, vinegar, coriander seeds, peppercorns, and salt in a pan with 1½ cups water and bring to a boil. Reduce the heat and leave to simmer for about 5 minutes.

Arrange the eggplant in a heatproof baking dish, pour the vinegar sauce over the top and leave to marinate for 2 to 3 hours, or overnight, in the fridge.

Remove the eggplant from the fridge 30 minutes before serving. Roughly chop the parsley leaves and scatter over the top of the dish when ready to serve.

★ Optional extra
Serve with boiled or steamed potatoes, some Savory Cashew Cream (page 150) or Saffron Aioli (page 106), and a green salad for a delicious Mediterranean-inspired meal.

SALT-BAKED BEETS & POTATOES WITH SAFFRON AIOLI

There's nothing better for a lazy chef than to put food in the oven and step back while it does all the work. This dish is a perfect example, and full of flavors inspired by Spanish and Southern French cuisine. It is also full of color, especially if you use different-colored beets and potatoes.

Serves 4

☆	☆	☆	☆	☆	☆
3 lb. (5 cups) coarse sea salt	1 lb. 10 oz. potatoes, preferably pink and purple	1 lb. 10 oz. fresh beets, preferably red, yellow and Chioggia	Pinch of saffron threads (about 20)	1 batch Savory Cashew Cream (see page 150) or plant-based yogurt	2 or 3 garlic cloves, chopped

Preheat the oven to 400°F.

Spread half the salt to cover the bottom of a baking sheet. Pierce each potato and beets a couple of times with a fork, then arrange them on the salt layer and cover with the remaining salt. Bake in the oven for about 1 hour until tender.

While the vegetables are cooking, make the aioli. Place the saffron threads in a cup and pour over 2 to 3 tablespoons boiling water. Leave to steep for 5 to 7 minutes. Remove the threads and purée the saffron water with the cashew cream and garlic cloves in a blender until smooth.

When the vegetables are cooked, shake off the excess salt and slice in half, then serve with the aioli, accompanied, if you wish, with a fresh green salad.

ZUCCHINI FRITTATA

One thing that always seems to thrive in my vegetable garden, no matter the weather, is zucchini. There's always an abundance of varying sizes, so the opportunities to experiment are endless. This frittata is a fantastic summer meal, particularly when served with a large tomato salad.

Serves 4

☆	☆	☆	☆	☆
2 medium zucchini, grated	2 garlic cloves, finely chopped	1 cup chickpea flour	¼ teaspoon turmeric (optional, for color)	Handful of chopped fresh basil

Preheat the oven to 350°F. Grease a baking sheet or line with parchment paper.

Cook the grated zucchini in a nonstick ceramic pan with 2 tablespoons water until soft. If the water evaporates before the zucchini is done, add a bit more. Stir in the garlic and continue to cook for an additional 3 to 4 minutes. Season to taste with salt and freshly ground black pepper.

Blend the chickpea flour with the turmeric (if using), a pinch of salt and 2 cups water in a large bowl until well combined and clump-free. Add the cooked zucchini and chopped basil to the batter and mix well. Pour the mixture into the baking pan and bake for 40 to 45 minutes.

Leave to cool for 10 minutes before slicing and serving with a fresh tomato salad.

★ Tip
Black Indian salt (kala namak) will give this dish an eggy taste.

SAVORY GALETTE

A *galette* in France is a rustic, open-faced free-form pastry. The dough is rolled out, the filling placed on top, and the edges are folded over the filling. If the dough tears or the filling leaks, that's fine — it's all about simplicity. This version calls for ground chia seeds or flaxseeds, which you can grind in a high-speed blender or using a pestle and mortar. The traditional oil is also swapped for tahini (or almond butter). You could save half the dough, wrap it in plastic, and keep in the fridge for up to 5 days or freeze it.

Serves 4 to 6 (makes 1 large or 2 small)

☆	☆	☆	☆	☆	☆
2⅓ cups spelt flour	4 tablespoons ground chia seeds or flaxseeds	½ cup tahini (sesame paste) or almond butter	5 lbs. 8 oz. red onions, peeled and sliced into rings	3 tablespoons Dijon mustard (or other spicy mustard)	Some sprigs of fresh thyme

Place the spelt flour, ground chia seeds or flaxseeds, tahini, and 1 teaspoon salt in a large bowl and mix together using a fork until the mixture is crumbly (with pea-sized lumps). Slowly incorporate ½ cup ice-cold water while gently kneading the dough. Be careful not to overwork it or it will become tough. Shape into a ball, wrap in plastic wrap and refrigerate for about 20 to 30 minutes.

Cook the onions in a large skillet with a splash of water over medium heat, adding more water as it evaporates. After 5 minutes add the thyme and continue to cook until the onion is soft and golden—about 20 minutes. Season to taste.

Preheat the oven to 400°F. Unwrap the dough and, using a rolling pin, roll it out between two pieces of parchment paper until it's a circle of about 15 inches. This can be a bit tricky because the dough can be quite crumbly, so if cracks appear simply take a piece of the dough from the outside and put it over the crack, then replace the parchment paper and roll over the area. (If you want to make 2 smaller ones, divide the dough in half and roll each out to a circle of about 8 inches.)

Spread the mustard on top of the dough and top with the onion filling, leaving 2 inches all around the edge. Fold this over the filling, using the paper underneath to help.

Carefully lift the galette onto a baking sheet and bake for about 35 minutes until the crust is golden brown. Serve warm or cold.

COCONUT-CRUSTED CRISPY PUMPKIN

As I learned more about healthy eating I stopped eating deep-fried food, but I liked that crispy taste so much that I wanted to recreate it in a healthier way. A two-layered coating of chickpea flour and desiccated coconut gives the best result. This is simple and cheap, and can be enjoyed either as a snack or as part of a Japanese-themed dinner.

Serves 8 to 10 for snacking

☆	☆	☆	☆	☆	☆	☆
1 pumpkin (e.g. red kuri)	1½ cups chickpea flour	1½ teaspoons granulated garlic	1 teaspoon ground ginger	1 teaspoon chili powder (use less for a milder version)	2½ cups dried coconut	Asian Sweet and Spicy Sauce (page 163) or tamari sauce, to serve

Preheat the oven to 400°F. Line a baking sheet with parchment paper.

Cut the pumpkin in half and remove the seeds and strands with a spoon. Peel or cut off the skin. Cut the flesh into wedges no thicker than ½ inch.

Place the chickpea flour, granulated garlic, ginger, chili powder, and 1 teaspoon salt into a large bowl and pour in 1½ cups water. Whisk vigorously until no clumps remain.

Spread the dried coconut out on a large plate. Take a pumpkin slice and dip it into the chickpea batter, making sure all sides are coated. Shake off the excess batter, then dip it into the dried coconut, ensuring it is thoroughly coated. Lay the coated slice in the prepared baking pan and repeat this process with all the pumpkin.

Bake in the oven for 16 to 20 minutes until the inside is soft and the outside turns golden brown. Eat warm with the Asian Sweet and Spicy Sauce.

SMOKIN' BURGERS

If you have some grains and beans already cooked then making vegan burgers is really easy. The key to a tasty burger is to make it with strong umami flavours. Here, the caramelized onions and miso paste ensure a deeply satisfying taste explosion.

Makes 4 to 6 burgers

☆	☆	☆	☆	☆	☆	☆
3 red onions, chopped, plus ½ onion sliced into rings	1½ cups cooked red kidney beans (14 oz., drained)	6 oz. cooked (3½ oz. dry) red rice	3 tablespoons fine oat flakes	1 tablespoon miso paste	1 teaspoon liquid smoke (or 1 teaspoon smoked paprika)	½ teaspoon chili powder (or more to taste)

Cook the onions in a pan on a medium heat with a splash of water until soft, golden and caramelized. If needed, add a little more water to prevent burning.

In a food-processor, blend the onions, beans, rice, oat flakes, miso paste, liquid smoke, and the chili powder well, but leave some structure.

Divide the mixture to form six even-sized balls and press them into round patties. If you have time, place them in the refrigerator to chill for 30 minutes or more.

Fry the patties in a little coconut oil for about 3 to 4 minutes in a skillet over medium–high heat on each side until golden and crispy. Serve topped with onion rings and optional extras of your choice (see below).

★ Optional extras

Although they're delicious on their own, these burgers are also great on a bun with some Ajvar (page 163) or Mustard Maple Sauce (page 160), avocado, or lettuce.

ZUCCHINI "CANNELLONI" WITH A PUMPKIN & SAGE FILLING

Pumpkin, sage, and almond ricotta make quite a classic flavor combination. Using zucchini ribbons, instead of pasta, makes this lighter and also gluten-free.

Serves 3 to 4

☆	☆	☆	☆	☆	☆	☆
1 pumpkin (approx. 2 lbs.) or 1½ lbs. pumpkin purée	2 lbs. 3 oz. fresh spinach (or use frozen spinach, defrosted)	2 large zucchini	14 oz. Almond Ricotta (page 146) or tofu, finely crumbled	2 tablespoons chopped fresh sage	¾ teaspoon freshly grated nutmeg	7 tablespoons nutritional yeast

If you are making your own pumpkin purée, preheat the oven to 400°F. Line a baking sheet with parchment paper.

Place the pumpkin on the baking sheet and roast in the oven for about 60 to 90 minutes (depending on your oven and the size and variety of pumpkin). Remove when a knife inserted in the skin goes in easily and smoothly. Leave to cool a little, then slice it in two, scoop out the seeds, and scrape out the flesh. You should have about 1½ lbs. cooked pumpkin (you can do this step in advance). Lower the oven to 350°C.

If you are using ready-made pumpkin purée, or have made it in advance, preheat the oven to 350°F.

Steam the spinach for 1 to 2 minutes and set aside. Cut the zucchini lengthways into thin ribbons using a mandoline or potato peeler. Work on one side of the zucchini until you reach the core, then from the other side. Discard the core.

Place the pumpkin purée and the almond ricotta in a large bowl and combine using a fork. Add the sage, nutmeg, nutritional yeast, and a good grinding of salt and freshly ground black pepper to taste.

Lay a zucchini ribbon on the work surface with the short end facing you. Place a tablespoon of the filling on the end of the zucchini ribbon, add some of the spinach and then roll the zucchini into a "cannelloni" and place it in a baking dish. Repeat until all are done. Sprinkle some whole leaves of sage over the "cannelloni" and cook in the oven for 45 to 50 minutes. Remove from the oven when done and serve.

INDIAN HAND PIES

Bitter garnituur are classic bar snacks in The Netherlands and often consist of cheese balls, meat or chicken, served with mayonnaise – not ideal for vegans! These Indian Hand Pies are the perfect substitute: they are full of flavor and much healthier than the classic Dutch fare. Make them in advance they'll be ready to serve whenever you have drinks with family and friends – eat them either on their own or with some yogurt or mango chutney.

Makes about 25 to 28

☆	☆	☆	☆	☆	☆	☆
2 cups whole-grain spelt flour	2 tablespoons nut butter	2 onions, chopped finely	2 teaspoons curry powder	½ to 1 teaspoon chili powder	3 oz. frozen peas, defrosted	11 oz. cooked sweet potato, cut into ½-inch cubes

Combine the spelt flour, nut butter, a pinch of salt, and ⅔ cups cold water in a large bowl and mix to form a dough. Shape it into a disc, but try not to overwork it. Wrap it in plastic wrap and refrigerate for at least 20 minutes.

Meanwhile, make the filling. Cook the onions in a large pan over medium heat with a splash of water for about 5 to 6 minutes, until translucent. Add the curry powder, chili powder, peas, and sweet potato, and gently stir so that you don't break up the potatoes too much. Add salt to taste. Transfer the mixture to a bowl and let sit.

Preheat the oven to 350°F and line a baking sheet with parchment paper. Remove the dough from the fridge and roll it out on a lightly floured surface to about 1/16 inch thick. Using an upturned glass or a cookie cutter, cut out rounds about 3 inches in diameter. Re-roll your scraps and repeat until all the dough has been used.

Place about 2 teaspoons of the filling in the center of each round. Using a pastry brush, brush a little water around the edge and then fold the circle in half and press the edges firmly together. Use a fork to make a decorative edge. Transfer each filled pastry to the lined baking sheet, and repeat until all the pastry is used. Bake in the oven for about 20 to 25 minutes, until golden brown.

Remove the hand pies from the oven and leave to cool slightly before serving.

SUSHI SANDWICH

We are all familiar with sushi, but have you heard of onigirazu? It uses the same components as sushi, but is shaped like a sandwich. Onigirazu is super easy to make, delicious, looks impressive, and is perfect for a packed lunch. Smoked Carrot Lax (page 50) and avocado make a vegan version of the popular California roll.

Makes 4 sandwiches (8 halves)

☆	☆	☆	☆	☆	☆	☆
7 oz. round rice (or 14 oz. cooked rice)	1 teaspoon brown rice vinegar	4 sheets of nori	½ cucumber, thinly sliced in rounds	1 serving of Smoked Carrot Lax (page 50)	2 tablespoons black sesame seeds	1 avocado

Cook the rice in 1¾ cup of water with ½ teaspoon salt according to the package instructions.

Remove it from the heat and sprinkle over the brown rice vinegar. Leave to cool until lukewarm.

Lay a large piece of plastic wrap on a flat surface. Place a nori sheet on top in a diamond shape, one tip facing you, with the smooth side facing down. With slightly damp hands, place a layer of rice, about ½ inch thick, in the center of the nori and form into a square of about 2½ inches (with one edge facing you).

Lay the toppings on the rice square. Start with the cucumber, then the Carrot Lax, a sprinkle of sesame seeds and some of the avocado slices. Finish with another layer of rice.

Now close the sandwich by folding the corners of the nori sheet over the filling. Start with the top and bottom ones, using the plastic wrap to help you. Stick the two corners together with a little water. Fold over the outer corners in the same way. Keeping the sushi sandwich in the plastic wrap, gently press down your sandwich so all ingredients stick together. Remove the plastic wrap if you are serving these sushi sandwiches right away, but keep it in place if you want to take them with you. Cut in half before serving.

★ Optional extras
Serve with some wasabi paste and tamari or nama shoyu.

☆ START ☆ FRESH ☆ FAST ☆ NOURISH ☆ GATHER ★ **SWEET** ☆ BASIC

APPLE TART WITH ALMOND CRUST

If there is one food tradition that everyone grows up with in the Netherlands, it has to be apple pie. The Dutch say that your home will sell more quickly if it smells of freshly baked apple pie. This is a delicious vegan, sugar-, and gluten-free version. With an added twist of French patisserie in the decoration, it becomes a fancy apple and almond tart.

Serves 8

☆	☆	☆	☆	☆	☆	☆
3 cups ground almonds	¼ teaspoon baking soda	3 to 4 tablespoons brown rice syrup	3 to 4 tablespoons almond butter	4 to 5 medium red organic apples, cored and thinly sliced	1 teaspoon cinnamon	2 tablespoons coconut sugar

Preheat the oven to 325°F.

In a large bowl, mix the ground almonds, baking soda, and a pinch of salt. Add 3 tablespoons rice syrup and 3 tablespoons almond butter and mix together with a fork (or pulse in a food-processor) until it looks clumpy but comes together when squeezed. If it's too dry, add another tablespoon each of rice syrup and almond butter.

Press the mixture into a lined 8½-inch tart pan with a removable bottom, ensuring it is distributed evenly. (The crust will be firmer if it is well pressed.)

In a large bowl, mix the apple slices with the cinnamon and coconut sugar, being careful not to break the slices. To make the apple rose, arrange the slices in the tart bottom from the outside in, overlapping the slices in a spiral, packing them tightly.

Place the tart in the oven and bake for 40 to 45 minutes until golden brown. Leave to cool and serve.

★ Optional extras
Eat the cake with Sweet Cashew Cream (page 150), whipped coconut cream, or Ice Cream (page 124).

THE BEST ICE CREAM

Most storebought ice creams (including vegan ones) are loaded with refined sugar, but these are a delicious and totally healthy alternative made mainly from fruit. Very ripe bananas make a perfect, naturally sweet base – just peel, slice, then freeze them. You can add all sorts of flavors to the basic recipe, such as the three suggestions below. Experiment with whatever chopped nuts, herbs, spices, or dried edible flowers you like. These can be eaten right away or stored in the freezer in an airtight freezerproof container for up to 2 months.

BASIC RECIPE

Makes about 4 cups

☆	☆	☆	☆
5 very ripe bananas, peeled, sliced and frozen	1½ cups other frozen fruit	¾ cup plant-based milk	A few drops of liquid stevia (for sweetness)

Remove the fruit from the freezer and allow to thaw for 5 minutes.

Place all the ingredients in a high-speed blender or food-processor and blend until smooth, scraping down the sides occasionally, if needed. When smooth, serve immediately.

STRAWBERRY AND BASIL ICE CREAM

Makes about 4 cups

☆	☆	☆	☆	☆	☆
5 very ripe bananas, peeled, sliced and frozen	1½ cups frozen strawberries	¾ cup Almond or Cashew Milk (page 146)	3 tablespoons chopped basil	A few drops of liquid stevia	1 teaspoon pink peppercorns, crushed

Remove the fruit from the freezer and allow to thaw for 5 minutes. Place all the ingredients in a high-speed blender or food-processor and blend until smooth, scraping down the sides occasionally, if needed.

When the mixture is smooth and creamy, serve immediately.

BLUEBERRY, LEMON, AND LAVENDER ICE CREAM

Makes about 4 cups

☆	☆	☆	☆	☆	☆
5 very ripe bananas, peeled, sliced, and frozen	1½ cups frozen blueberries/ wild blueberries	3/4 cup almond or cashew milk (page 146)	1 tablespoon dried lavender	Juice of 1 lemon	A few drops of liquid stevia

Remove the fruit from the freezer and allow to thaw for 5 minutes.

Place all the ingredients in a high-speed blender or food-processor and blend until smooth, scraping down the sides occasionally, if needed.

BANANA AND WALNUT ICE CREAM WITH CARAMEL SAUCE

Makes about 4 cups

☆	☆	☆	☆	☆	☆
10 very ripe bananas, peeled, sliced and frozen	A few drops of stevia	¼ cup chopped walnuts	1½ cups (5 oz.) pitted Medjool dates	3 tablespoons almond butter	¼ teaspoon sea salt

Remove the bananas from the freezer and leave to thaw for 5 minutes.

Place in a high-speed blender or food-processor with the stevia and blend until smooth, scraping down the sides occasionally, if needed.

Transfer the ice cream into a freezerproof container and mix in the chopped walnuts. Freeze until ready to serve.

Place the dates, almond butter, salt, and ½ cup water in a high-speed blender and process until smooth. If it's too thick, add a little more water, 1 tablespoon at a time, until you reach your desired texture.

When you are ready to serve, spoon a little ice cream into a glass and pour over some of the sauce, repeating as many times as you want for a layered result.

RASPBERRY & LEMON MUFFINS

At the height of summer, when berry season arrives, my daughter loves to stuff her mouth full of ripe berries. And it's not only her; the birds love them, too. So if I want to make something with berries, I have to be in the garden at the break of dawn to beat them. I gather and freeze raspberries them until I have enough to use; frozen berries have the advantage of staying in shape when stirred into the muffin batter. They're also a great way to introduce a little sunshine into your home in winter months, if you can resist them for that long!

Makes 10 to 12

☆	☆	☆	☆	☆	☆	☆
2⅓ spelt flour	½ teaspoon baking powder	½ teaspoon baking soda	1¼ cup Homemade Yogurt (page 151) or coconut yogurt	1/2 cup maple syrup	Zest of 1 lemon and juice of ½ lemon	½ cup frozen raspberries

Preheat the oven to 350°F.

Sift the flour into a large bowl with the baking powder, baking soda, and ¼ teaspoon salt.

In another bowl, mix together the yogurt, maple syrup, lemon zest and juice, then pour this into the bowl of dry ingredients and mix together. Stir in the frozen raspberries.

Distribute the batter between the cups of a muffin pan (I like to use a silicone mold that doesn't need greasing). Bake for 20 to 25 minutes until a toothpick inserted in the middle comes out clean.

Leave to cool a little before eating.

CAROB CAKE WITH STRAWBERRIES & BLACK PEPPER

Carob pods come from the carob tree, which grows in the Mediterranean. Although used as a substitute for chocolate, it has a different flavor: more caramelly and nutty. It's mostly sold as a powder, and is naturally sweetened and caffeine free. Pairing carob with fresh strawberries and black pepper gives this raw cake an extra bit of oomph!

Serves 6–8

☆	☆	☆	☆	☆	☆	☆
1¼ cup raw walnuts	10 Medjool dates, pitted and chopped	4 medium ripe avocados	¼ cup maple syrup	4 tablespoons carob powder	1 teaspoon vanilla extract	8 to 10 strawberries

Blitz the walnuts with a pinch of salt in a food-processor until it reaches flour consistency. Be careful not to overdo it or you will end up with nut butter.

Add the dates and process some more until a ball forms. Press the mixture into the bottom of a 8 1/2 inch-diameter cake pan with a removable bottom, ensuring that you distribute it evenly. Place the pan in the fridge while you make the filling.

Halve the avocado and take out the pit. Scoop out the flesh and add to the bowl of the food-processor together with the maple syrup, carob powder, vanilla extract, and a pinch of salt. Process until smooth.

Remove the walnut–date base from the fridge and spread the avocado mixture over the base. Chill the cake in the freezer for 2 to 3 hours.

Meanwhile, cut the strawberries into quarters. Remove the cake from the freezer 10 to 15 minutes before serving, to make it easier to slice, then arrange the strawberries on top of the cake in the center. Grind some black pepper on top and serve. When you slice the cake, clean your knife between each cut you make.

★ Variation

For a chocolate version, substitute the carob powder with the same amount of cocoa powder. You can also change the fruit depending on the season; strawberries, cherries, or raspberries are good in summer, while pomegranate, oranges, or figs are great for winter.

RAW CARROT CAKE

My favorite juice has to be carrot, but they leave a lot of pulp when juiced. This recipe transforms carrot pulp into a delicious raw cake, and so helps avoid waste. Unlike a lot of raw cakes, this is not loaded with nuts so it leaves you light and fulfilled after eating.

Serves 6 to 8

☆	☆	☆	☆	☆	☆	☆
9 oz. carrot pulp (or grated carrot, squeezed tightly in a dishcloth to remove as much juice as possible)	¾ cup raisins	5 Medjool dates, pitted	Zest of 1 organic orange (or use lemon zest)	1 tablespoon ground cinnamon	1 cup dried coconut flakes, plus extra for topping	Sweet Cashew Cream (page 150) or whipped coconut cream

Line a 8½-inch removable bottom cake pan with plastic wrap.

Process all the ingredients in a food-processor until well combined, then spread the mixture into the cake pan. Press the mixture in well so it is firm and even. Chill in the fridge for about 1 hour.

Spread the sweet cashew cream on top and sprinkle with a thin layer of coconut flakes, then serve.

★ Tip
You can make the cake a day in advance, as it will improve in flavor when left to sit in the fridge.

FRUIT CRUMBLE WITH ALMOND & STAR ANISE TOPPING

A hot fruit crumble is a delicious seasonal treat. Make it with whatever fruit the current season is providing and add your favorite spices. Star anise pairs beautifully with the pears and blackberries here, but you could also add cinnamon, cardamom, vanilla, or even herbs like thyme to the crumble topping.

Serves 4 to 6

☆	☆	☆	☆	☆	☆	☆
5 pears, peeled, cored and roughly chopped	5 plums, pits removed, cut into quarters	1 cup blackberries	3 cups ground almonds	1¼ fine oat flakes	5 tablespoons maple syrup	1½ teaspoons ground star anise

Preheat the oven to 300°F.

Mix the fruit together and place them in an ovenproof dish (approximately 8 x 10 inches).

Combine the ground almonds, oat flakes, maple syrup, and star anise in a bowl and mix with a fork until crumbly. Spread the crumble mix evenly over the fruit and bake for 30 to 35 minutes in the oven. Be careful that the crumble topping does not burn; if it browns too fast, just cover the dish with a piece of foil.

Remove the crumble from the oven and serve.

★ Optional extras
Serve with some Ice Cream (page 124), Sweet Cashew Cream (page 150), or Homemade Yogurt (page 151) on top.

CRISPY ALMOND COOKIES

This recipe delivers all you could want from a cookie. They're made with ground almonds and almond flakes, ensuring a great crunch after baking.

Makes 15 cookies

☆	☆	☆	☆	☆	☆
1½ cups ground almonds	¼ cup almond flakes	5 tablespoons maple syrup	3 tablespoons almond butter	1 tablespoon arrowroot	1 teaspoon vanilla extract

Preheat the oven to 300°F and lay some parchment paper on a clean, even surface.

Combine all the ingredients in a large bowl and mix with a fork until crumbly, then keep mixing until it holds together. Collect the dough into a ball and transfer it to the parchment paper. Place another piece of parchment paper on top of the dough, then use a rolling pin to roll on top of the paper, flattening and widening the dough. Continue until it is ¼-inch thick, then use a cookie cutter or glass to cut out the cookies.

Carefully transfer the cookies to another baking sheet lined with parchment paper. Bring together the remaining cookie mixture and repeat the process until all your cookie dough is used. Bake for 8 to 10 minutes until golden brown, but keep an eye on them because they burn quite easily.

After the cookies are done, take them out of the oven. Let the cookies cool so that they can become crisp. Keep the cookies in an airtight container.

★ Optional extra

Although these cookies are perfect as they are, they're also delicious served as two waffles with ice cream (see page 124) in the middle.

SUNFLOWER BUTTER FUDGE

This fudge is full of flavor and one of the most indulgent and easy to make sweet treats. Make it in advance and keep it in the freezer so you can have this treat on the table within minutes.

Makes 24 squares

☆	☆	☆	☆
1 cup sunflower seed butter	⅓ cup maple syrup	5 tablespoons cacao or carob powder	1 teaspoon vanilla extract

If your seed butter is very stiff, remove it from the jar and gently warm it in a pot on a low heat. Transfer to a food-processor, add the remaining ingredients and a pinch of salt, and blitz until the mixture forms a balll.

Line a square baking dish with plastic wrap. Press the fudge into the dish, distributing it evenly, then chill in the refrigerator for at least an hour.

Sprinkle a thin layer of cacao or carob powder on top using a fine mesh strainer.

Carefully remove the fudge from the dish and transfer it to a plate. Remove the plastic wrap before cutting the fudge into 1-inch squares.

★ Variations
You can use any seed or nut butter you want, or instead of the cacao powder, you can use some coarse sea salt flakes, coconut flakes, chopped nuts, or freeze-dried raspberries. Gently press these in before chilling the fudge in the refrigerator.

APRICOT "PROFITEROLES"

I really enjoy being inspired by classic dishes and giving them a healthy twist. These Apricot "Profiteroles" use a delicious apricot instead of the classic choux pastry ball, and whipped coconut cream in place of the traditional dairy version. This coconut cream is also great in other recipes, too – it's vital to use a coconut cream or milk without additives or thickeners, and chill it for 1 to 2 days before whipping; otherwise you won't get the stiff result you are looking for in a whip.

Makes about 16 to 20

☆	☆	☆	☆
2 x 14 oz. cans full-fat coconut milk or coconut cream	2 to 3 tablespoons maple syrup, brown rice syrup, or stevia	1 teaspoon vanilla extract	16 to 20 ripe apricots

Refrigerate two cans of coconut milk or cream for 1 to 2 days before you plan to make the dessert.

Open the cans and scoop out the solidified coconut into a bowl. Reserve the coconut water for use in another recipe, such as a smoothie. Add the sweetener, vanilla, and a pinch of salt to the coconut and whip with a fork or a hand mixer until fluffy and smooth. Transfer the mixture to a piping bag if you have one.

Gently cut open each apricot from top to bottom on one side along its natural line and remove the pit. Pipe some of the coconut cream into the apricot or fill using a teaspoon. Repeat until all are done, then serve.

ROSE YOGURT WITH BERRIES & CARAMELIZED PISTACHIOS

This dessert sounds really fancy, but it's very simple to make. Pink peppercorns are, in fact, not a pepper, but a berry from the Peruvian pepper tree, which is related to the cashew family. Their aroma is rosy and sweet with some punch, and they are very delicate easily crushed with a knife. Serve these indulgent treats in individual cups and impress your guests.

Serves 4 to 6

☆	☆	☆	☆	☆	☆	☆
2½ cups Homemade Yogurt (page 151) or coconut yogurt	3 teaspoons rosewater	2 to 3 drops stevia or other sweetener	2½ cups mixed red berries	1 tablespoon pink peppercorns, crushed	1 cup raw shelled pistachios, roughly chopped	1 tablespoon brown rice syrup

Line a tray or plate with parchment paper.

Mix the yogurt in a bowl with the rosewater and sweetener. Place the berries in another bowl, sprinkle over the pink peppercorns, and gently stir them in.

Heat a nonstick ceramic pan over medium heat and gently toast the pistachios, stirring. Add the brown rice syrup and let it bubble for about 30 to 40 seconds, then spread the caramelized pistachios out on the paper-lined tray or plate and leave to cool and become crisp.

Divide the berries between individual cups or glasses, spoon over the yogurt, and top with the caramelized pistachios.

LEMON COCONUT PANNA COTTA WITH ORANGE

This recipe is very versatile and has been in my repertoire for many years. You could also use it as a filling for a cheesecake, or blend it to make a pudding. Panna cotta is traditionally milk-based and thickened with gelatin, but this version uses coconut milk and is stiffened with agar agar and arrowroot. Agar agar is a seaweed substitute for gelatin and arrowroot is a gluten-free thickening agent that is a relative of ginger root. Try this with segments of blood orange, blackberries, blueberries, cherries, or grilled peaches instead of oranges.

Serves 4

☆	☆	☆	☆	☆	☆	☆
2¼ coconut milk	Zest of 1½ lemons and juice of 1 lemon	1 ½ teaspoons agar agar powder	8 to 10 drops of liquid stevia	1 tablespoon arrowroot	2 oranges, segmented with skin and membrane removed	Some mint or rosemary as a garnish

Combine the coconut milk, the lemon zest and juice, and the agar agar powder in a pot and bring to a gentle boil over low heat. Add about 8 drops of stevia and taste to see if it is sweet enough for your liking. Add some more if not. Whisk vigorously and often to prevent clumps on medium heat for about 5 to 6 minutes.

Dissolve the arrowroot in 3 tablespoons water in a small bowl, then add to the coconut milk. Stir well to thicken and ensure there are no lumps. Cook for about 1 minute.

Remove from the heat and divide between four bowls, then place the bowls in the fridge for 2 to 3 hours.

Just before serving, remove from the fridge and gently turn the panna cotta out onto individual serving plates. Arrange the orange segments, or any seasonal fruit, on top of the panna cotta and sprinkle over some of the mint or chopped rosemary and serve.

★ Variations
To make a vanilla version, omit the lemon and add one teaspoon of powdered vanilla.
To make a chocolate version, omit the lemon and add 3 tablespoons of cacao.

☆ START | ☆ FRESH | ☆ FAST | ☆ NOURISH | ☆ GATHER | ☆ SWEET | ★ **BASIC**

ALMOND MILK, "RICOTTA" & CURD

Making nut milk is a daily ritual in my home: we drink it plain, warmed, or mixed with granola. Fortunately, it's pretty straightforward to make. Soak the almonds in water and peel them to take away their bitter taste, or use blanched nuts. The leftover pulp is beautifully white and can be used to make "ricotta," which you can use in Zucchini "Cannelloni" with a Pumpkin and Sage Filling (see page 114) and Filled French Bread (see page 102). The "ricotta" also freezes well.

ALMOND MILK

Makes 4 cups

☆	☆
1 cup unblanched almonds, soaked overnight	2 to 4 tablespoons maple syrup or 2 pitted dates

Blend the almonds with a pinch of salt and 4 cups water in a high-speed blender for about a minute, until smooth. Strain the milk through a nut-milk bag or strainer lined with fine cheesecloth. Reserve the nut pulp for making almond "ricotta" (see below).

If you want to sweeten the milk, add the maple syrup or dates. It will keep for 3 to 4 days in the fridge.

ALMOND "RICOTTA"

Makes ¾ cup

☆	☆	☆	☆
¾ cup almond pulp (see above)	4 cups Almond Milk (see above)	3 tablespoons Homemade Yogurt (page 151)	2 teaspoons nutritional yeast

Mix all the ingredients together thoroughly in a bowl with a pinch of salt (for savory use). This is best used right away or the next day. (If it smells bad, has a pink tint or colored spots, throw it away.)

You can easily add flavor with lemon juice, a tablespoon of white miso, garlic, chopped fresh herbs, or even some liquid smoke. To make a sweet version, add maple syrup, vanilla extract, or ground cinnamon.

ALMOND CURD

Once you have made your own almond milk, it's really easy to make almond curd. It's a bit like cottage cheese or paneer and, although it doesn't hold its shape as well as, it is a delicious substitute for regular soft cheese.

Makes about ¾ cup

☆	☆	☆
4 cups almond milk	Juice of ½ lemon	3 tablespoons nutritional yeast (optional)

Heat the almond milk in a pot over medium heat until lukewarm and add the lemon juice while stirring. Turn off the heat, cover the pot with a lid and leave to cool to room temperature for 45 to 60 minutes.

Line a strainer with a piece of cheesecloth, pour in the almond mixture, and place it over a bowl. Bring together the four corners of the cheesecloth and tie together to form a bag. Hang this over the bowl for a couple of hours so the whey can drip through the cheesecloth, leaving the curd.

Mix the curd with a pinch of salt and the nutritional yeast if you intend to use it in a savory dish, or with a sweetener, fresh fruit, or spices such as vanilla or cinnamon to use in a dessert or a baked tart.

Store the curd in the fridge for a maximum of 4 days. (If it smells bad, has a pink tint, or any colored spots, throw it away.)

★ Serving suggestion
This can be rolled into cheese balls, mixed with grain dishes, salads, or simply used as a spread on your bread.

ALMOND "FETA"

A lot of people on a vegan diet miss cheese. I have experimented with alternatives a lot, and in the course of my research I came across a recipe for almond feta in Miyoko Schinner's *The Homemade Vegan Pantry*, in which steeping the cheese in brine creates that authentic feta flavor. This is my take on vegan feta, and although it takes some time to make, it's delicious, very versatile, and will soon become a kitchen staple. The agar agar powder helps the mixture set; it's a vegan gelatin made from seaweed.

Makes about 12 oz.

☆	☆	☆
¾ cup blanched ground almonds	1 tablespoon apple cider vinegar	1 tablespoon agar agar powder

Place the ground almonds, apple cider vinegar, ½ teaspoon salt, and 1 cup water in a high-speed blender and blend until smooth.

Place the agar agar powder and ⅓ cup water in a pot over a low heat, whisking firmly until bubbles form. Turn the heat to low, put the lid on and simmer for 2 to 3 minutes.

Remove the lid and mix in the almond mixture well using a whisk. Pour the mixture into a square heat-resistant plastic mold lined with plastic wrap or a silicone mold. Leave to cool completely; it will take a couple of hours.

Make the brine by stirring 3 tablespoons sea salt into 4 cups freshly boiled water until the salt has dissolved. Pour the brine into a container with a lid and leave to cool completely.

Place the almond block into the cooled brine and leave to age in the fridge for 3 to 4 days for optimum taste.

This almond "feta" should keep for 10 days in the fridge. If it smells funny, has a pink color or shows grey patches, it has gone bad; throw it away and make a new batch.

CASHEW CREAM

This smooth sauce is so versatile that it can be made savory or sweet; add fresh herbs and garlic for a nice dip, thin it and use as a creamy salad dressing, mix with extra nutritional yeast to make a lovely cheesy sauce, or add chili for a spicy mayonnaise. Mixing in vanilla maple syrup will make the perfect topping for a cake, or pair it with fresh fruits and granola to make a parfait. There are endless possibilities. Be creative!

SAVORY CASHEW CREAM

Makes about 2¼ cups

☆	☆
1½ cups raw cashews, soaked overnight and rinsed	1 tablespoon apple cider vinegar or the juice of ½ lemon

Place the cashews, vinegar, 1 teaspoon salt, and ⅔ cups water in a high-speed blender and blitz until very smooth. If you want the cream to be more liquid, add a tablespoon of water at a time to thin it out. Add other flavorings of your choice.

Store the cream in a glass container in the fridge for a maximum of three days.

SWEET CASHEW CREAM

Makes about 2¼ cups

☆	☆	☆
1½ cups raw cashews, soaked overnight and rinsed	3 to 4 tablespoons of stevia or other sweetener	½ teaspoon vanilla powder extract or the seeds of ½ vanilla pod

Place all the ingredients into a high-speed blender with ⅔ cup water and blend until very smooth. If you want the cream to be more liquid, add a tablespoon of water at a time to thin it out.

Store the cream in a glass container in the fridge for a maximum of three days.

HOMEMADE YOGURT

When I'm in rural France, the nearest place to buy my favorite vegan organic yogurt is 45 minutes away, so I created this homemade version. Knowing that yogurt is basically fermented milk with live cultures added to it, I decided to experiment by mixing coconut milk with a probiotic capsule and putting it in a yogurt maker. This attempt was a failure, but by adding soaked cashews and a thickener it was a success! If you have a yogurt maker or a dehydrator this will speed things up, but it's not necessary. In summer, the yogurt will develop more quickly due to the warmer weather.

Makes about 3¼ cups

☆	☆	☆	☆
¾ cup raw dry cashews (soaked overnight and rinsed)	1½ cups coconut milk	½ teaspoon tapioca powder	½ cup plant-based yogurt (e.g. coconut yogurt)

Blend the cashews and coconut milk together in a high-speed blender until very smooth. Transfer the mixture to a pot, add the tapioca powder and bring to a gentle boil while whisking well to incorporate the tapioca. Leave to simmer for 2 minutes, stirring from time to time, until thickened. Leave to cool to 108°F, then remove the thin layer that will have formed on top of the mixture. Add the yogurt or probiotics (see below) and blend again in a high-speed blender.

Place the mixture in a yogurt maker, or in a bowl in a dehydrator, and leave for 6 to 8 hours. Alternatively, pour the yogurt into a clean, sterilised glass container, covered with a piece of muslin or cheesecloth, in a warm place (but not direct sunlight). It will develop in 24–48 hours. Small bubbles will start to appear and it will smell and taste lightly sour like real yogurt.

When ready, store in the fridge for up to 4 days.

★ Variations
For a lighter version, replace the coconut milk with 1 cup almond milk (or other nut milk) and 1 cup water. You could also swap the plant-based yogurt for 2 capsules vegan probiotics (2 teaspoons probiotic powder).

SWEET & SALTY CASHEWS

These cashews are so irresistible I have to watch out that my daughter doesn't eat them all too quickly. They can be eaten as a snack, but they're also super delicious added to a salad or in an Asian-style dish like the Asian Stir Fry on page 61.

Serves 4–6 as a snack

☆	☆	☆	☆	☆
1 tablespoon maple syrup	1 tablespoon nama shoyu or tamari	1 teaspoon garlic powder	1 teaspoon smoked ground paprika (optional)	1½ cups raw cashews

Preheat the oven to 350°F and line a baking sheet with parchment paper.

In a small bowl, mix the maple syrup, nama shoyu, or tamari with the garlic powder and smoked paprika, if using. Place the cashews in a large bowl, pour over the sauce, and mix well until thoroughly coated.

Transfer the cashews (leave the excess seasoning in the bowl) to the lined baking sheet, spread out evenly, and roast in the oven for 3 minutes.

Remove the sheet, stir the nuts then return them to the oven and cook for a further 3 to 4 minutes. Keep an eye on them: they should turn light golden, but you don't want to burn them.

Remove the nuts from the oven and allow to cool so they become crisp, then serve.

★ Variations
You can add all sorts of additional flavors to the spice mix: curry powder, ground cinnamon, five-spice powder, ground ginger, etc. Experiment and make this recipe your own! You could also substitute the cashews for a mix of nuts, e.g. walnut, almond, cashew, etc.

BASIC TOMATO SAUCE

Our local farm has an incredible variety of beautiful ripe tomatoes available to pick, including heritage ones, big "coeur du boeuf," small cherry tomatoes (which are tempting to eat right away), yellow, purple, and green ones. These tomatoes are fantastic in salads, because they are so fresh and tasty, but they are also perfect for making a delicious sauce. It can be used as a base for pizza, pasta, or any other recipe that calls for tomato sauce.

☆	☆	☆	☆	☆	☆	☆
2 lbs. 3 oz. ripe tomatoes	1 large onion, chopped	2 to 4 garlic cloves, finely chopped	1 to 2 teaspoons maple syrup, to taste	3 tablespoons balsamic vinegar	1 tablespoon chopped fresh herbs (optional)	½ teaspoon chili powder (optional)

Start by removing the skin from the tomatoes. The best way to do this is to cut a little cross on the bottom of each tomato, place them in a large pot of simmering water for about 30 seconds, then take them out and plunge them in a bowl of cold water. The skin should have loosened so you can peel them easily, then roughly chop the flesh.

Cook the onions in a pot over medium heat with a splash of water until they are transparent and lightly golden, about 5 minutes. Add the tomatoes, garlic, maple syrup, balsamic vinegar, fresh herbs, salt and chili (optional).

Bring to a boil with the lid on, then reduce the heat to low and leave to simmer for 35 minutes. Taste for seasoning and add more salt if needed.

★ Tip
Try fresh oregano, thyme, rosemary, or basil to flavor the sauce.

VEGETABLE STOCK

Soup is great for using up all your leftover vegetables, grains, and beans and creating a really tasty bowl! In France, dinner is still sometimes referred to as *souper*, which basically means to eat soup. Like a lot of good dishes, soup has to start with a great base: a good stock. This really flavorful veggie stock is a great start for a lot of homemade soups, but also a perfect base for a risotto or other sauces.

☆	☆	☆	☆	☆	☆	☆
2 onions, unpeeled	6 stalks of celery, roughly chopped	4 medium carrots, roughly chopped	9 oz. mushrooms	4 to 5 sprigs of thyme	1 head of garlic, cut in half horizontally	1 bay leaf

Place all the ingredients in a pot large enough to give you room to stir everything and pour over enough water to cover the vegetables. Bring to a boil, then reduce the heat to low and leave to simmer for 40 to 60 minutes. (The longer you leave it to simmer, the more intense the flavors will be.)

Remove the vegetables from the stock. If you want a clear broth, you can pass it through a strainer lined with cheesecloth.

★ Variations
You can use all sorts of vegetables, herbs, and spices in your stock. Try the following: tomatoes, leeks, celery root, parsnip, chiles, dried mushrooms, fennel, beets, rosemary, sage, coriander seeds, allspice seeds, mace.

HERB & LEMON CHICKPEA CROUTONS

Roast chickpeas add bursts of flavor and texture. Serve over salads, soup and grain bowls, or enjoy as a snack. To get the chickpeas crispy, put them in a hot oven.

☆	☆	☆	☆	☆
2½ cups drained cooked chickpeas (2 x 14 oz. cans)	2 teaspoons dried rosemary	2 teaspoons dried thyme	2 teaspoons garlic powder	Juice and zest of 1½ lemon

Preheat the oven to 400°F (fan-assisted) and line a baking sheet with parchment paper.

Dry the chickpeas and remove any loose skins. Combine in a large bowl with the remaining ingredients and ½ teaspoon salt (to taste). Stir until well coated.

Spread on the lined baking tray and cook for about 25 minutes, shaking occasionally.

NORTH AFRICAN-STYLE CHICKPEAS

Chickpeas have a very subtle taste, so can be easily paired with all kinds of flavors. Curry powder or garam masala, to salt and vinegar, there are endless possibilities. Try experimenting with your favourite combinations.

☆	☆	☆	☆	☆	☆
2½ cups cooked chickpeas (2 x 14 oz. cans)	1 teaspoon ground cumin	1 teaspoon ground coriander	1 teaspoon ground smoked paprika	½ teaspoon dried ground fennel	1 teaspoon garlic powder

Preheat the oven to 400°F (fan-assisted) and line a baking sheet with parchment paper.

Drain the chickpeas, reserving a little liquid, then dry and remove any loose skins. Combine in a large bowl with the remaining ingredients, ½ teaspoon salt and 3 tablespoons of the reserved liquid. Stir until well coated.

Spread on the lined baking sheet and cook for about 25 minutes, stirring occasionally.

HUMMUS TWO WAYS

Hummus truly is an all-round player – on sandwiches, as a dip, as part of a mezze meal, with a salad, or as a sauce. Cook a big batch of chickpeas and store them in the fridge or freezer ready for use. Experiment with the spices and garlic in these recipes. The green hummus has almost the same taste as falafel.

BASIC HUMMUS

Makes about 3 cups

☆	☆	☆	☆	☆	☆
2½ cups cooked (2 x 14 oz. cans) or 1¼ cup dried chickpeas	1 piece kombu (if you cook the chickpeas yourself)	3 garlic cloves, chopped	¼ cup tahini	Juice of 1 lemon	1 teaspoon ground cumin

To cook your own chickpeas, soak the dried beans for 8 to 10 hours or overnight, then rinse and place them in a large pot with the kombu and plenty of water. Add salt at this stage will toughen the skins. Bring to a boil, skimming off the foam that appears on top. Cook for 1 to 1½ hours until the chickpeas are soft but keeping their shape.

Mix the garlic, tahini, lemon juice, cumin, ½ teaspoon salt, and 1 cupwater in a blender, then add the drained chickpeas and process until very smooth. You might need to scrape down the sides from time to time. If the mixture is too thick for your liking, add a little more water. Taste and add additional seasoning if needed.

GREEN AND SPICY HUMMUS

Serves 2 to 3

☆	☆	☆	☆	☆	☆
1 batch Basic Hummus (see above)	¼ cup fresh parsley, chopped	¼ cup fresh cilantro, chopped	¼ cup fresh mint, chopped	3 oz. spinach, chopped	½–1 teaspoon chili powder

If you want to cook your own chickpeas, follow the method for Basic Hummus above. Blend all the ingredients together with ¼ teaspoon salt and 1 cup water in a blender until smooth. Store in the fridge for up to 4 days.

OIL-FREE DRESSINGS

A great dressing can really lift a salad or transform a dish, but they're often packed full of fatty oils which I like to avoid. Although it may seem strange not to include oil, you won't miss it in these delicious dressings. Here are a few of the best recipes.

LEMON TAHINI DRESSING

This is delicious combined either with a Middle Eastern-themed meal, a fresh green salad, steamed greens, or warmed through with pasta and vegetables. If you want to turn it into a dip, simply reduce the quantity of water.

Makes about 1 ½ cups

☆	☆	☆
⅓ cup tahini	Juice of 1 lemon	1 garlic clove

Blend all the ingredients together with ¼ teaspoon salt and 1 cup water in a blender until smooth.

Store in the fridge for up to 4 days.

MUSTARD MAPLE SAUCE

This is fantastic with a simple green salad or grain bowl, or even as a dip with steamed artichokes or roasted vegetables.

Makes about 2 cups

☆	☆	☆	☆
1½ cups Savory Cashew Cream (page 150) or plant-based yogurt	3 tablespoons mustard	2 tablespoons maple syrup	1 tablespoon apple cider vinegar

Blend all the ingredients with ½ teaspoon salt in a blender until smooth.

Store in the fridge for up to 4 days.

ASIAN SWEET AND SPICY SAUCE

This spicy, sweet-and-sour sauce uses Thai flavors. Use as a dip, in stir-fries, or as a marinade.

Makes about 1¾ cup

☆	☆	☆	☆	☆
1 cup brown rice syrup	1 cup apple cider vinegar or rice vinegar	3 garlic cloves, chopped	Thumb-sized piece of ginger, grated	3 to 5 fresh red chiles, chopped

Place all the ingredients, with ½ teaspoon salt and 1 cup water, in a blender and mix until combined but not smooth: you should still see pieces of chile. Place in a pan over a medium heat and bring to the boil. Reduce the heat and cook for 20 minutes, until reduced and thickened.

Remove from the heat and cool. Pour into a sterilized jar and store in the fridge for of 2 weeks.

AJVAR

In the Balkans this relish is traditionally made to spice up winter dishes. It's great on toast with avocado, mixed in a Mediterranean-style salad, or on a veggie burger – it's like a smoky ketchup.

Makes about 2¼ cups

☆	☆	☆	☆	☆
5 red peppers	2 medium eggplants	2 garlic cloves, chopped	1 teaspoon ground hot smoked paprika or chili powder	3 tablespoons apple cider vinegar

Preheat the oven to 475°F. Line a baking sheet with parchment paper.

Place the vegetables on the baking sheet and roast until the skins are blackened. Transfer the peppers to a bowl and cover with plastic wrap to soften the skins. When cool, peel and deseed the peppers and halve the eggplant, scooping out the flesh. Purée both in a blender.

Put the purée in a pan over medium heat and add the remaining ingredients with a pinch of salt. Bring to a boil, then reduce and simmer for 10 minutes, stirring often. Remove from the heat and leave to cool. Pour the Ajvar into a clean jar and store in the fridge for up to a week.

PICKLES

The tangy flavor and crisp texture of pickles lift any meal. Hard root vegetables are best, such as carrots, onions, beets, and cabbages. Or mature zucchini that are much harder than young ones. A mandoline helps to slice the vegetables, although if they are too thin they'll turn soggy. Spices are also great flavor boosters: mustard seeds, coriander seeds, cumin seeds. You can experiment with different vinegars, too; apple cider vinegar, mixed 50–50 with water, is sour but not too strong.

RADISH, FENNEL AND ONION

This delicious pickle turns a beautiful shade of pink after one day of pickling.

Makes about 2 pint jars

☆	☆	☆	☆
1 bunch of radishes, sliced into rounds	1 medium fennel bulb, core removed, thinly sliced	2 red onions, thinly sliced	1 cup apple cider vinegar

Combine all the vegetables in a large bowl and add 1 teaspoon salt. Mix everything together with your hands, then pack the mixture tightly into three 1½ cup jars. Pour about ⅓ cup of vinegar into each jar so it reaches halfway up the jar. Boil some water and pour this into the jars to almost fill them. Seal the jars and give them a shake so that the liquids are well combined. Store in the fridge for at least 1 day before using. The pickle is best eaten within 1 week after opening.

SPICY CUCUMBER

This pickle makes a great accompaniment to Asian-inspired meals.

Makes about 2 pint jars

☆	☆	☆	☆	☆
1 cucumber	2 shallots, sliced in rings	1 chile, chopped in slices	3 tablespoons rice vinegar	1 teaspoon rice syrup

Cut the cucumber in half lengthways. Scoop out the seeds and slice each half into thin half moons. Place these in a bowl together with the shallots, chile, rice vinegar, rice syrup, and 1½ teaspoon salt.

Mix well, cover the bowl with plastic wrap and leave for at least 30 minutes. Pack into jars with lids if you like. You can also leave it overnight in the fridge, where it will keep for 2 to 3 days.

MY PANTRY

The best way to ensure you can create wonderful, delicious food at any moment is to have a well-stocked pantry. The recipes in this book include some ingredients that may be unfamiliar to you, but most you can get from your local organic store or supermarket. Other, more unusual ones, such as Indian black salt and liquid smoke (see page 169), you can order online.

The following are essentials in my pantry.

Beans

Normally I cook my own beans, but if I'm in a hurry, I will use a jar or a can. Make sure that your can is BPA-free, though. I stock many different types of beans, including:

Chickpeas

Red and yellow lentils

French Puy, black beluga and brown lentils – Leep their shape while cooking, have a delightful taste, and are best if they still have some bite to them. Ideal for salads.

Red kidney beans

Cannelini or lima beans

Frozen peas, green beans, and fava beans

Sprouted beans – Packed with nutrients. Green mung beans are ideal for sprouting.

Tempeh and tofu – I use bean-derived products sparingly, mostly in Asian dishes or as an egg substitute. Make sure they are organic and non-GMO.

Grains and pasta

Like beans, grains are a staple in the vegan or plant food diet. Pair them with nuts, seeds, and vegetables and you have a perfect protein-rich meal. Due to their slow release of sugars into the bloodstream whole grains will keep you satisfied for a long time. They also contain fiber, minerals, and vitamins. All grains need to be washed before you cook them. There are so many delicious grains out there to try, including:

Rice – Round brown, long-grain, black, and red rice.

Quinoa – Has a light, nutty taste and is a great gluten-free alternative.

Rolled oats – Daily in oatmeal, cookies, granola, and other sweet treats. (If you are gluten intolerant, checking the label: they can be cross-contaminated with wheat.)

Other gluten-free grains – Millet, millet flakes, buckwheat (which in fact isn't a grain but a seed). Sometimes I buy other grains like freekeh, spelt, barley, corn (for making my own popcorn), or polenta.

Pasta – Wholegrain pastas, such as spelt or rice pastas, and rice or buckwheat noodles.

Flours and Baking products

I stock a variety of gluten-free flours to bake with and other essentials for baking. My pantry includes the following:

Chickpea flour – Used in both Indian and Mediterranean cuisine, it is super versatile, has a slight nutty taste and can act as an egg replacer in many dishes. It is very high in protein and can be mixed with other gluten-free flours such as rice or buckwheat flour.

Blanched almond flour – Wonderful in cakes and I keep it in the fridge because of its high oil content.

Oat flour – I usually make it myself by grinding the flakes in a blender, then use it in cookies or mix it with almond flour to make pastry.

Chestnut flour – Made by grinding dry chestnuts and common in Italy and France, it has a mildly sweet and nutty taste. Combines well with buckwheat flour or polenta.

Whole-grain spelt – for fast bread making.

Other essentials for baking – Baking soda and aluminum-free baking powder, to give my baking some lift; arrowroot, as a thickener and binder. I use it instead of cornstarch and as an egg substitute in baking, too.

Nuts and Seeds

Nuts and seeds are essential in my cooking, but because they contain such a high amount of natural fats I usually limit myself to one handful a day. Store them in a dark place, or even in your fridge, to prevent the oils turning rancid. My favorites are:

Almonds – Super versatile and the only nuts to have an alkalinizing effect on the body. If you have a strong food-processor it is easy to make almond butter: just let the machine run for about 10 to 12 minutes with the s-blade.

Cashews

Walnuts – I like to forage my own.

Pistachios

Flax seeds – Contain the highest plant source of omega 3. They are a great alternative to egg and are especially good for binding baked dishes. Mix 1 tablespoon of ground flax seed with 3 tablespoons of warm water, leave for about 15 minutes and you have yourself a flax egg!

Chia seeds – These "superseeds" also contain a lot of omega 3 and can also be used as an egg substitute. I use them to thicken liquid, make chia jam (see page 23) and add to smoothies or oatmeal.

Sesame seeds – very high in calcium, they come in black, brown, and white.

Sunflower seeds

Pumpkin seeds – real nutritional powerhouses, containing a lot of protein, zinc, iron, and omega 3.

Coconut – I always have coconut flakes, dried coconut, and a can of coconut milk in store. Use full fat coconut milk and ensure it contains only coconut and water.

Sweeteners

I don't use any refined commercial sugars at all, but, although I am not fond of processed food and like to eat food that is as natural as possible, I do use a variety of "natural sweeteners," including:

Maple syrup – Make sure you buy organic and pure maple syrup that doesn't contain added sugar, caramel, or high corn fructose syrup.

Coconut nectar and sugar – This doesn't taste like coconut and is less sweet than maple syrup. It has a slight caramel flavor, so I substitute it for brown or cane sugar.

Brown rice syrup – Also less sweet than maple syrup, brown rice syrup becomes more solid and gives a crunchy bite when heated, whereas maple syrup remains sticky.

Stevia – A herb that doesn't contain any sugar at all, this has no effect on your blood sugar. There are several forms available, the purest of which is ground green stevia powder. I buy liquid stevia, which is a combination of water and powdered stevia. You only need a couple of drops to sweeten your smoothies, ice creams, or desserts.

Dates – I prefer Medjool dates, which are naturally soft and quite large.

Carob powder – From the pod of the carob tree native to the eastern Mediterranean, carob powder is naturally sweet, contains no caffeine (unlike chocolate), no gluten, and a lot of fiber and antioxidants.

Banana purée and unsweetened apple sauce – Both provide natural sweetness and can be used in baking cakes, waffles, and cookies as a binder instead of egg.

Condiments and flavorings

Salt – Choose sea salt that has been sun dried, as commercial salts are heated, which destroys all their minerals. Add salt at the last moment to assure a real taste, and be carefully not to add too much. My favorites are Celtic sea salt from France and kala namak (Indian black salt), an unrefined salt that, due to high sulphur content, has the smell and flavor of hard-boiled eggs. It is very rich in umami flavor and great in dishes like quiches, savory cashew cream, and tofu scramble (see page 27). Find it in Indian or Asian stores or online. I also love truffle salt, which contains small dried pieces of black truffle, and smoked Danish salt, which gives a mild smoky flavor.

Miso – A salty, fermented paste, typically made from rice, barley, or soy beans, water and salt. Miso contains healthy cultures and vitamin B and has a rich umami flavor. Add at the last moment to stocks, soups, and sauces. Miso comes in different colors—the lighter version has a milder taste than darker (aged and saltier) miso pastes.

Nama shoyu – An unpasteurized soy sauce that add a deep and salty flavor.

Tamari – A soy sauce that doesn't contain wheat. Buy unpasteurized soy sauces;

commercial ones are heated, which results in them losing bacteria and enzymes.

Vinegar – My favorite is raw apple cider vinegar. Choose an organic, unfiltered, naturally fermented and unpasteurized one. You can use it over vegetables roasted in the oven as a substitute for oil. Brown rice vinegar, with its fresh and mild taste, is great for Asian-flavored foods.

Dried porcini mushrooms – Soak in hot water for 15 to 30 minutes and use the soaking liquid in your dish as well.

Mustard

Nutritional yeast – A vegan's dream, this flaky stuff has a savory "cheesy" flavor and is packed with minerals and nutrients. I use it in a raw "cheese" (see page 146) and in Savory Cashew Cream (see page 150).

Sun-dried tomatoes – I prefer the dry ones to the ones in a jar with oil. Soak them first or simply chop and add to stocks, stews, and sauces for extra depth of flavor. You can also use them as a substitute for tomato paste.

Olives – look for ones cured in sea salt and avoid ones that are artificially colored and contain preservatives.

Seaweeds – These real superfoods are a rich source of minerals, vitamins, and protein. I use kombu when boiling beans, or making stock. Nori sheets are ideal for making vegan sushi. Dried powdered nori gives a bit of fish flavor to my quinoa patties on page 66. And I use agar agar, a vegan substitute for gelatin, in desserts.

Liquid smoke – A seasoning that will give your dish a smoky flavor without the need for a smoke oven. Choose one that contains only water and a natural smoke flavour, store it in a dark place and remember that a little goes a very long way! If you can't find liquid smoke, you can substitute it with smoked paprika or smoked Danish salt.

Spices and Herbs

I use a lot of spices and herbs in my dishes. With their specific flavors and aromas, you can easily create dishes from Mexican to Indian, and from Nordic to Mediterranean. The most useful spices are chili, cinnamon, whole and ground coriander, whole and ground cumin, fresh ginger, smoked pimenton (smoked paprika powder), saffron, star anise, turmeric, and vanilla. Vanilla extract often contains added sugar, so I always use vanilla beans and vanilla powder instead. I also have ready made spice blends in my pantry, such as baharat, ras el hanout, garam masala, curry powder, five spice and herbes de Provence, just to name a few.

You will also find organic rosewater and orange blossom water in my cupboard. Rosewater is used mostly in sweet treats—ice creams, cookies, or drinks— in Middle Eastern and Indian cuisine. Spray rosewater over red fruits (like raspberries and strawberries), rhubarb or plums to give them a more floral note, but don't overdo it, or your dish will taste soapy. Orange blossom water is a great aromatizer in desserts, cakes, and smoothies and pairs beautifully with all orange fruits, such as oranges, apricots, peaches, and mangos. It is also delicious combined with carrots, pumpkin, nuts (almond, coconut, pistachio) and spices like cinnamon and anise.

Fresh herbs can really enliven dishes. My favorites include:

Basil, which combines well with: Artichokes, arugula, asparagus, beets, peppers, broccoli, capers, carrots, corn, eggplant, fava bean, fennel, garlic, green beans, leeks, lemon, marjoram, mushrooms, nectarines, olives, oregano, pasta dishes, parsley, parsnip, peaches, pine nuts, peas, pumpkin, radicchio, radishes, raspberry, samphire, strawberry, thyme, tomatoes, watercress, and zucchini.

Cilantro, which combines well with: Allspice, apple, apricot, beets, peppers, bok choy, broccoli, carrots, cauliflower, celery, chickpeas, chili, Chinese cabbage, chives, coconut milk, corn, cucumber, cumin, curry powder, dates, fennel, fresh beans, garlic, ginger, grapefruit, kaffir lime leaf, leek, lemon, lentils, lime, mango, mint, noodles, oranges, pineapple, plums, pumpkin, radicchio, radishes, red cabbage, rice, sweet potato, tomatoes, turmeric, watercress, and zucchini.

Dill, which combines well with: Anise, asparagus, arugula, basil, beans in general, beets, peppers, bok choy, Brussels sprouts, cabbage (Chinese, white, red and savoy), capers, caraway, carrots, cauliflower, celeriac, celery, chives, chestnut, coriander, corn, cucumber, cumin, eggplant, fennel, garlic, ginger, green peas, horseradish, mint, mustard, leeks, oregano, onion, parsley, pumpkin, radicchio, sauerkraut, spinach, and tomatoes.

Mint, which combines well with: Apple, almond ricotta, basil, beets, blackberry, black currant, black pepper, cabbage, cardamom, carrot, chamomile, cherry, chickpeas, chili, chocolate, cilantro, citrus fruit in general, coconut, cranberry, cucumber, cumin, ginger, green salad, dill, eggplant, fennel, fig, garlic, grape, guava, juniper, lavender, lemongrass, lentil, mango, marjoram, melon, nectarine, nutmeg, onion, papaya, pasta dishes, pea, peach, pear, pineapple, pomegranate, plant based yogurt, potatoes, radishes, raspberry, rhubarb, rice dishes, rosemary, sesame seeds, star anise, strawberry, summer rolls, tabbouleh, tahini, tarragon, tomatoes, thyme, watermelon, white beans, and zucchini.

Parsley, which combines well with: Artichoke, arugula, asparagus, basil, bay leaf, broad beans, cabbage in general, carrots, cauliflower, celeriac, chilli, chervil, chives, cucumber, dill, eggplant, garlic, grain dishes, green beans, kohlrabi, leeks, lemon, marjoram, mushrooms, mustard, onions, oregano, parsnip, pasta dishes, peas, potatoes, pumpkin, radicchio, radishes, rosemary, tomato and tomato based sauces, salad greens, salsa, sauerkraut, savory, sorrel, stocks and soups, and tarragon.

COOKING WITHOUT OIL

Eating wholefoods means eating food in its most original state, so I choose to eat nuts, seeds, avocados, and olives rather than their extracted oils, simply because they are easier for the body to digest.

I use 2 to 3 tablespoons of water or stock instead of oil, added to a hot pan. Using a nonstick ceramic pan is another way to avoid adding oil. To roast vegetables, I use white balsamic vinegar (which won't color your food), lemon or orange juice, water or stock. Add 2 to 3 tablespoons of liquid for a tray of vegetables.

To make super-crunchy potato chips, boiling potato wedges for 2 minutes, then place them on a lined baking sheet and turn your oven to the fan option. This will dry out the surface of the potatoes, leaving them crunchy on the outside and cooked inside. You can also mimic deep-fried crunchiness with a batter of chickpea flour, water and spices, rolled in dried coconut, ground almond flour, or fine breadcrumbs and then baked in the oven.

When baking, use silicone molds, which don't need oiling, or line baking sheets with parchment paper. Oils can be substituted with fruit purées such as mashed banana or unsweetened apple sauce. I also use nut butters, such as almond butter, or mixed tofu as an oil substitute.

INDEX

Rita is a Dutch recipe developer, food blogger and photographer. After following various cooking trends, she derived her own plant-based, seasonal and healthy style. She lives between The Netherlands and France with her husband and young daughter, experimenting with new ideas and vibrations in the quick, busy city life of Amsterdam and enjoying a quiet life tending her vegetable garden in the French countryside.

ACKNOWLEDGEMENTS

Writing a book is not a thing you do alone. It takes a lot of people to make a book from beginning until end. Firstly I want to thank my loving husband Dick. He supports me, helps me with testing recipes, gives me feedback and he always tells me to chase my dreams! Of course I thank my daughter Olivia, the light of my life, always curious and happy to taste all the things I make for her. She is truly one of the reasons for being focused on cooking healthy and plant based. She is part of a new generation that hopefully will be healthier and more kind to our planet. And I do not want to forget my parents who gave me a healthy start in life.

A big thanks to Claire, Hannah, Judith and Kyle at Kyle Books for making my dream of having my own cookbook come true. Without your support, feedback and beautiful work this book would not be here!

Also, I want to thank the wonderful team that put this book together. They have made it look so incredibly gorgeous with beautiful photography and design. Much appreciation for the work that you all did Laura, Tabitha, Kendall and Joss, I have fun memories of the short time we spent together, as well as Georgia for her fantastic design and Anne for her meticulous copy-editing.

I am grateful that I could use beautiful and timeless ceramics, made with lots of attention and detail by Annemieke Boots (www.annemiekebootsceramics.nl) and Jook (www.itsajook. com). Thank you for using your products. My food looks fantastic on your work! I would also like to mention the people of "By Mölle" (www.bymolle.com) that provided me with gorgeous handmade table linen, all handmade and sustainable.

A special thanks goes out to the large Instagram foodie community that gives me inspiration, support and love.

In general I would like to thank my friends and family that supported me in my cooking adventures and are always curious and happy to eat my food.

But most important are you that have bought my book. Hopefully it helps you eating more plants in a delicious way on a daily basis.